Open Learning Guide

Microsoft® Outlook® 2013

Release OL365v1

Published by: CiA Training Ltd

                 Business & Innovation Centre

                 Sunderland Enterprise Park

                 Sunderland

                 SR5 2TA

                 United Kingdom

                 Tel: +44 (0) 191 549 5002

                 Fax: +44 (0) 191 549 9005

                 Email: info@ciatraining.co.uk

                 Web: www.ciatraining.co.uk

                 ISBN: 978-0-85741-143-3

This guide was written for *Microsoft Office 2013* running on *Windows 8.x*. If using a different version of *Windows* some features and dialog boxes may look and function slightly differently to that described.

Windows 8.x and *Office 2013* are optimised to work with touch-screen controls. However, this guide assumes you are using a traditional mouse and keyboard. If not, allowances may need to be made.

A screen resolution of *1024x768* is also assumed. Working at a different resolution (or with an application window which is not maximised) may change the look of the dynamic *Office 2013 Ribbon*. For example, if space is restricted, a group of buttons may be replaced by a single button which, when clicked, will display the full group.

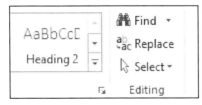

First published 2014.

Open Learning

CiA Training's *Open Learning Guides* are a comprehensive collection of structured exercises designed to teach, enhance and instil confidence in the use of popular software packages.

Software and data files

Microsoft Outlook 2013 is part of the *Microsoft Office 2013* suite of applications. This guide assumes that the program has been fully installed on your computer. Some features described in this guide may not work correctly if the program was not fully installed.

Downloading the data files:

Data files accompanying this guide allow you to learn and practise new skills without the need for lots of data entry. These files must be downloaded from the Internet. Go to **www.ciatraining.co.uk/data** and follow the simple on-screen instructions.

<u>Your *FastCode* for this guide's data is: **OL365**</u>

The data files should be installed in the following location on your computer:

Documents \ DATA FILES \ Open Learning \ Outlook 2013

Aims and objectives

This self-teach guide will provide you with the knowledge and skills necessary to make best use of e-mail software to safely and securely send, receive and store e-mail messages. It contains exercises covering the following topics:

- Opening & Closing *Outlook*
- Understanding & Using *Outlook*
- Creating E-mail Messages
- Sending Messages
- Receiving Messages
- Replying to Messages
- Forwarding Messages
- Sending/Receiving Attachments
- Creating Automated Responses
- Printing Messages
- Using a Signature

- Organising E-mail
- Using Contacts
- Creating Appointments
- Organising Meetings
- Creating Tasks and Notes
- Searching for E-mail
- Flagging Messages
- Use E-mail Safely
- Professional Considerations
- Guidelines, Laws & Procedures

Notation used throughout this guide

- Key presses are included within angled brackets. For example, <**Enter**> means press the **Enter** key.

- The guide is split into individual exercises. Each exercise usually consists of a written explanation of a specific learning outcome (*Guidelines*) followed by a number of stepped instructions for you to perform (*Actions*).

Recommendations

- Work through all of the exercises in this guide in sequence so that one feature is understood before moving on to the next.

- Read the whole of each exercise before starting to work through it. This ensures understanding of the topic and prevents unnecessary mistakes.

This guide is suitable for:

- Any individual wishing to learn how to use *Outlook 2013* to compose, send, receive and organise e-mail messages and calendar appointments. No prior knowledge of *Outlook 2013* is required.

- Tutor led groups as reinforcement material. It can be used as and when necessary.

Contents

Section 1

Getting Started

By the end of this section you should be able to:

Understand Basic E-mail Principles

Start and Close Outlook

Recognise and Use the Outlook Screen

Find Help

Exercise 1 - E-mail and Outlook

Guidelines:

One of the most popular uses of the Internet is sending and receiving "electronic mail" (**e-mail**). E-mail is an extremely important communication tool that allows people to send multimedia messages to other ICT users anywhere in the world *instantly*. Think about how much more quickly information can be sent using e-mail rather than by traditional surface or airmail.

This guide will introduce you to *Microsoft Outlook*, a popular **Personal Information Management** (**PIM**) tool that allows you to send, receive and organise e-mail messages. *Outlook* can also be used to attach files to messages, maintain an address book of contacts, and create useful calendars and to-do lists.

Note: *There are many online services that you can use to send and receive e-mail. However, in most professional situations, a Personal Information Management tool such as* Outlook *is used.*

Before you can use *Outlook* (or any other e-mail program or service), you will first need your own e-mail address. In the same way that a phone number uniquely identifies an individual telephone on a network, your e-mail address uniquely identifies your "mailbox" on the Internet (i.e. the location where all of your e-mail is delivered).

E-mail addresses all follow the same general format, as the following example shows:

trainer@bigplanetsupport.co.uk

Note: *The @ symbol is pronounced "at" and is used to separate a person's mailbox name (which can include full stops, e.g. john.smith) from the name of their organisation or Internet Service Provider (ISP). Notice that this matches the organisation's or ISP's* **domain name***.*

Note: *If you do not know your* <u>own</u> *e-mail address, contact the person who runs your computer network. If you are a home user, contact your ISP.*

When you are not using *Outlook*, messages are stored for you until they are collected. You do not need to keep the program running all of the time.

Actions:

Food for thought:

1. There are approximately 3.3 billion e-mail users in the world. In 2012, they sent around 144 billion e-mails every day!

2. Do you know what your own e-mail address is? If you don't know it, ask the company or service that provides your e-mail.

Exercise 2 - Starting Outlook

Guidelines:

Microsoft Outlook is an e-mail program that is part of the *Microsoft Office* suite of applications. Although there are numerous ways to start the program, the following method is recommended for beginners.

Actions:

1.   Display the *Windows* **Start Screen** if it is not already open.

Note: The **Start Screen** *can be opened by clicking the* **Start** *button in the bottom left corner of the* **Desktop***. If using an earlier version of Windows, click* **All Programs** *on the* **Start Menu** *to show a list of available apps.*

2.   Locate the e-mail app **Outlook 2013**. You may need to scroll down or right to find it.

Note: *You can also type* **Outlook** *on the* **Start Screen** *(or* **Start Menu***) to search for the* **Outlook** *app.*

3.   Click **Outlook 2013** once. The app starts.

Note: *Outlook may need to be configured before it can be used for the first time. Configuring is the term used to describe the supply of initial user information to the program. If the* **Internet Connection Wizard** *or* **Add New Account** *dialog box appears when you start* **Outlook***, contact your IT Administrator or Internet Service Provider who will be able to help you configure the program.*

Note: *When you start Outlook you may first be asked to connect to the Internet – you need to do this to send and receive e-mail. Also, if there is more than one e-mail account (profile) available on the computer, you will need to select one.*

Exercise 3 - The Outlook Window

Guidelines:

When the *Outlook* window appears, the program will display your **Mail** view. All of your e-mail messages are contained here in folders known as your **mailbox**.

Actions:

1. Examine the *Outlook* window and locate the **Ribbon**, **Tabs**, **Folder Pane**, **View Buttons**, **Message List**, **Reading Pane** and **Status Bar**.

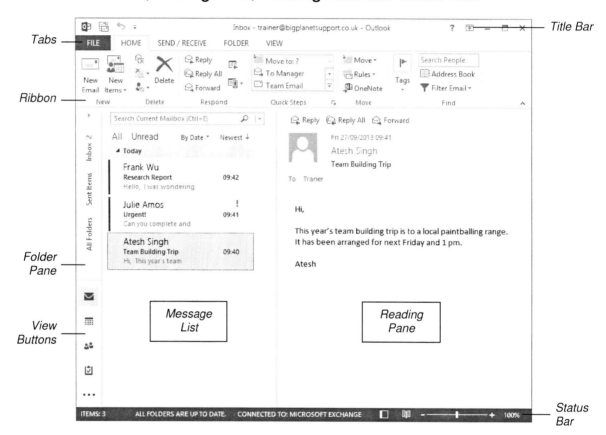

Note: Don't worry if your screen does not appear exactly as shown above. Outlook features a wide variety of layouts and set-up options. You will learn how to adjust basic display settings in the next exercise.

2. Notice that **Mail**, ⬛, is the currently selected view button at the bottom of the **Folder Pane**. If it is not, click it once to select it now.

3. Locate the **Message List**. This shows all of the messages currently contained in the selected folder on the **Folder Pane** (e.g. **Inbox**). If this is the first time you have used *Outlook*, the list will probably be empty.

4. Locate the **Reading Pane**. The content of any message selected in the **Message List** is previewed in the **Reading Pane**.

Note: You can adjust pane sizes by dragging the boundary bar between them.

Exercise 3 - Continued

5. Locate the **Ribbon**. This consists of a range of tabs containing buttons organised into groups.

6. The buttons on the **Ribbon** are used to select an action or command in *Outlook*. Move the mouse pointer over any button but do not click. Read the **ToolTip** that appears which gives the name of that button and a small description.

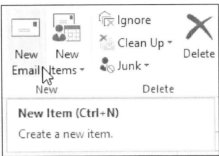

7. Click each tab in turn and examine the various features available. When you are finished, return to the **HOME** tab.

Note: *The* **FILE** *tab contains a list of basic program functions such as* **Info**, **Open & Export**, **Save As**, **Print** *and* **Exit**. *More advanced e-mail account and* Outlook *options can also be accessed from here.*

8. At the top left of the screen is the **Quick Access Toolbar**, . Identify the two useful buttons that are available here: **Send/Receive All Folders** and **Undo**.

9. Find the **Status Bar** which runs along the bottom of the *Outlook* window. This displays messages as tasks are performed. It will currently show the total number of messages (or **ITEMS**) in your **Inbox**.

10. Notice the **Zoom** slider to the right side of the **Status Bar**. This can be used to increase or decrease zoom levels in the **Reading Pane**.

Note: *By default, the* **Zoom** *level is set to* **100%**. *However, if you find it difficult to read text in the* **Reading Pane**, *feel free to "zoom in" at any time.*

11. Leave the *Outlook* window open for the next exercise.

Exercise 4 - Outlook Views

Guidelines:

There are many different views available in *Outlook*, but perhaps the most important is your **Mail** view.

Note: *To match the screenshots in this guide, it is recommended that you set up* Outlook *using the following instructions. When using* Outlook *for real, however, you can choose whichever screen layout you feel is most useful.*

Actions:

1. Display the **VIEW** tab on the **Ribbon**.

2. Then, in the **Layout** group, click the **Folder Pane** drop-down button. From the options that appear, select **Off** and observe the effect. The **Folder Pane** is hidden.

3. Click the **Folder Pane** drop-down button again and select **Normal**.

4. Next, click the **Reading Pane** button in the **Layout** group. Select the **Off** option and observe the effect. The **Reading Pane** is hidden.

5. Click the **Reading Pane** button again and select the **Bottom** option.

6. To adjust your screen's **Mail** layout to match this guide's recommended settings, click the **To-Do Bar** button and select **Off**. Then click the **Change View** button in the **Current View** group and select **Single**.

i *Your view should now match that shown below. You will learn more about the **To-Do Bar** in a later exercise.*

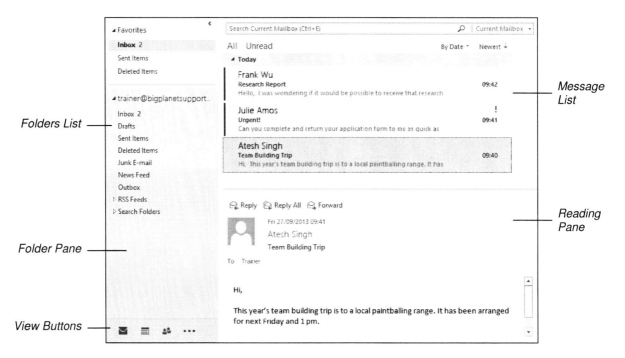

Exercise 4 - Continued

7. Examine the **Folders List** which contains a list of mailbox folders (i.e. **Inbox**, **Outbox**, **Junk E-mail**, etc). You will get the opportunity to explore these in more detail as you progress through this guide.

Note: *If you are using a web-based e-mail provider, your folders may appear grouped under the service's name (e.g.* 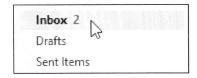*). If this is the case, simply expand this folder to view your entire mailbox.*

8. If your **Inbox** folder is not currently selected, click it once now.

Note: *All messages that you receive are placed in your **Inbox** folder. A number after the folder name indicates how many <u>unread</u> items are present.*

9. Next, to hide the **Ribbon**, click the **Ribbon Display Options** button, ⌹, shown at the top-right of the *Outlook* window (on the **Title Bar**).

10. Examine the options available and then select **Show Tabs**. Only the **Ribbon's** tabs are now shown – this gives you a little more room to work in.

Note: *Clicking a tab will briefly display the full **Ribbon** again.*

11. To restore the **Ribbon** to its original size permanently, click the **Ribbon Display Options** button again and select **Show Tabs and Commands**.

12. Next, click the **People** view button, ⛷, found towards the bottom of the **Folder Pane**. This view can be used to access and organise your "contact" information – details about friends, family, colleagues and business contacts.

Note: *It is likely that there is no contact information shown here at the moment. Later exercises will show you how to create new contacts.*

13. Next, click the **Calendar** view button, ▦, on the **Folder Pane**. This view can be used to plan your daily activities and schedule appointments and meetings with other people.

14. Finally, click the **Mail** view button, ✉, to return to your mailbox.

Exercise 5 - Outlook Help

Guidelines:

Outlook contains a very useful and comprehensive **Help** facility. If you forget how to use a feature of the program or encounter an unexpected problem, this extra source of information will be very useful.

Help topics are available from either **Office.com** (via the Internet) or from the content installed on your computer (offline). The method of using **Help** is the same in either case but the content may vary slightly.

Actions:

1. Click the **Microsoft Outlook Help** button, ?, found to the far right of the **Title Bar**, to display the **Outlook Help** window.

*Note: Pressing the <F1> key will display the same **Outlook Help** window. The window can be moved, resized or maximised if required.*

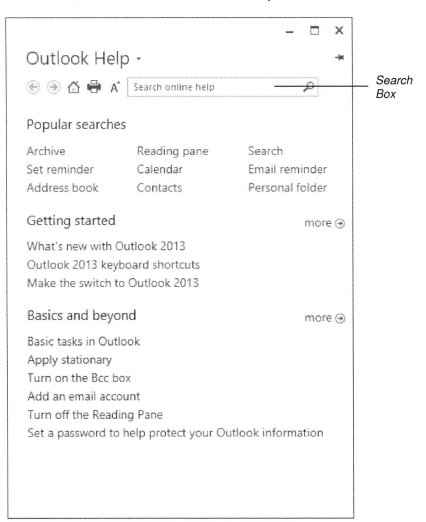

*Note: As the help screen downloads live content from **Office.com**, the contents may not appear exactly as shown above.*

Exercise 5 - Continued

2. A list of **Popular searches** is shown on the opening screen. Click on any one that is of interest to you to display a list of relevant topics.

3. Scan the topics shown and select any one that you find interesting. Read the help information shown.

4. To move back to a previous screen, click the **Back** button, 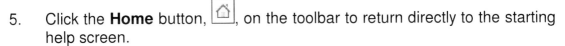, on the **Outlook Help** toolbar. You are then able to follow another link.

Note: *Help topics can be printed for reference by clicking the **Print** button,* 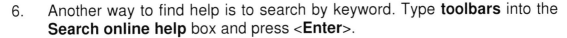.

5. Click the **Home** button, 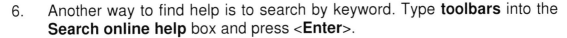, on the toolbar to return directly to the starting help screen.

6. Another way to find help is to search by keyword. Type **toolbars** into the **Search online help** box and press <**Enter**>.

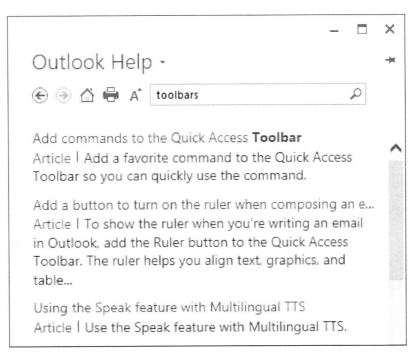

Note: *There may be many topics found for your search and it will be necessary for you to use your own judgement and select the most appropriate one.*

7. Scan the topics found and again select any one that interests you. Read the help information shown.

8. Try searching for information on **keyboard shortcuts**. Find an appropriate article and read the useful information shown.

9. When you are finished, click the **Close** button, 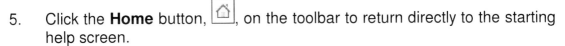, on the **Outlook Help** box to close it (not the close button on the **Outlook** window).

Exercise 6 - Closing Outlook

Guidelines:

Outlook can be closed at any time. In some instances you may also need to terminate your Internet connection (if you are using a dial-up connection, for example) if no prompt to disconnect appears automatically.

When *Outlook* is not running, incoming messages will continue to be received and held for you, either by your Internet Service Provider or your organisation's server (a computer that manages your network). When you next connect, all waiting messages will be passed to your mailbox.

Note: You do not need to keep Outlook *running all of the time. You will not miss or lose any messages that you receive when* Outlook *is closed.*

Actions:

1. Click the **Close** button on the **Title Bar** at the top right of the *Outlook* window.

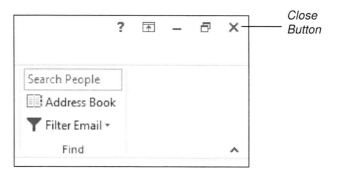

*Note: Alternatively, display the **FILE** tab and select **Exit**.*

2. *Outlook* is now closed. Any new e-mail message that you receive will be held for you by the organisation that provides your e-mail service.

*Note: If you are using a dial-up connection and the **Auto Disconnect** dialog box does not appear, click the **Network** icon, 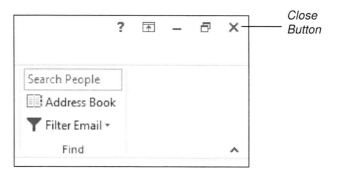, in the **Taskbar Notification Area**, select your dial-up connection, and then click **Disconnect**.*

Exercise 7 - Revision

Guidelines:

At the end of every section you get the chance to complete one or more revision exercises to develop your skills. You should aim to complete the following steps without referring back to the previous exercises.

Actions:

1.   Start *Outlook*.

2.   What is a PIM?

3.   How is the @ symbol in an e-mail address pronounced?

4.   What always follows the @ symbol in an e-mail address?

5.   *Outlook* features a variety of different "views" such as **Mail**, **Calendar**, and **Contacts**. How can you switch between these?

6.   What is your **Inbox** folder used for?

7.   What is the **Message List** used for?

8.   What is the **Reading Pane** used for?

9.   Minimise the **Folder Pane**.

10.   Hide the **Ribbon** (**Show Tabs**) and turn off the **Reading Pane**.

11.   Restore the **Ribbon** (**Show Tabs and Commands**).

12.   Set the **Reading Pane** back to **Bottom**.

13.   Restore the **Folder Pane** back to **Normal**.

14.   Before continuing, make sure **Folder Pane** is set to **Normal**, the **Reading Pane** is set to **Bottom** and the **Ribbon** is visible.

15.   Close *Outlook*.

Note: Sample answers can be found at the back of the guide.

Section 2

Send & Receive

By the end of this section you should be able to:

Compose a New E-mail Message

Address an E-mail

Send an E-mail

Receive an E-mail

Mark an E-mail as Read/Unread

Exercise 8 - Creating a Message

Guidelines:

Using e-mail to send information is an extremely efficient way to communicate with other people. All you need is the e-mail address of the **recipient** (i.e. the person you are sending the message to).

Note: Always be careful when you enter an e-mail address. One letter out of place will result in the message being returned "undelivered" or – even worse – going to the wrong person.

Actions:

1. Start *Outlook*. When the *Outlook* window opens, the **Mail** view should appear automatically with the **Inbox** folder selected.

2. Locate the **New** group on the **Ribbon** (make sure the **HOME** tab is displayed). Click the **New Email** button to start a new message.

3. An **Untitled Message** window appears.

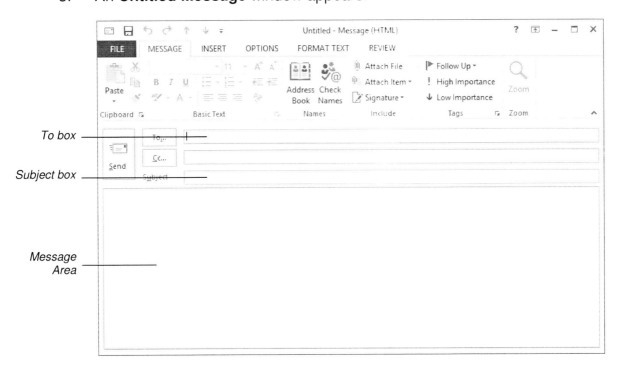

*Note: To give you more space to work in, you can maximise the **Untitled Message** window (i.e. make it fill your entire screen) by clicking the **Maximize** button, , on the window's **Title Bar**.*

4. Maximise the new message window now (if it is not already).

5. Notice that the cursor is currently flashing in the **To** box (if it is not, click inside the **To** box now). The **To** box is where you enter the e-mail address of the person you are sending the message to.

Exercise 8 - Continued

Note: *Entering your own e-mail address in the **To** box will cause any message you send to be immediately returned to you. This allows you to observe the results of sending messages. Sending a message to another person follows exactly the same steps.*

6.   Type <u>your own</u> e-mail address into the **To** box.

Note: *When instructed to enter your <u>own</u> e-mail address, enter the address of the mail account that you are currently using with Outlook. If you don't know it, ask the company or service that provides your e-mail.*

7.   Click once in the **Subject** box. The text you enter here is used to briefly describe the content of your e-mail (allowing the recipient to see at a glance what the message is all about).

Note: *It is good practice to <u>always</u> enter a short but relevant subject for every new message that you create.*

8.   Enter the following subject text: **My First Message**.

Note: *The e-mail address **trainer@bigplanetsupport.co.uk** will be used in screenshots throughout this guide. Wherever relevant, you will be prompted to substitute this with your own e-mail address.*

9.   Click once in the **Message Area**. Notice that the title of the e-mail, shown on the **Title Bar**, now changes to **My First Message**.

10.   Type the following text into the **Message Area**:

I am sending this e-mail message as part of my studies.

Note: *If you make a spelling mistake when typing it will be underlined in red. You will learn more about correcting spelling errors in the next section.*

11.   Leave the new e-mail message open for the next exercise.

Exercise 9 - Sending a Message

Guidelines:

When you have finished composing (writing) a new e-mail, the message is ready to be sent. Copies of sent messages are stored in the **Sent Items** folder for you to refer back to later.

Note: *Depending on how Outlook is set up, the **Sent Items** folder may appear with a slightly different name (e.g. **Sent Mail**). If this is the case, you will need to use that folder in place of **Sent Items**.*

Actions:

1.   The e-mail created in the previous exercise (**My First Message**) should still be open. You are now going to send it.

Note: *It is always a good idea to check the content of e-mail messages before you send them to ensure address, subject and message text are all correct. Once an e-mail is sent, there is very little you can do to get it back again.*

2.   Click the **Send** button to send the message to the recipient (yourself in this case).

Note: *If you receive a prompt to correct spelling errors in your message, click **Cancel**. Checking e-mail for spelling errors is covered in a later exercise.*

3.   The e-mail window closes and the message is sent to your **Outbox**.

Note: *E-mail messages that you send are first moved to your **Outbox** folder before being sent. If you are connected to the Internet, they will be sent immediately from there. If you are not, messages will remain in your **Outbox** – this way you can create e-mail messages "offline" and then send them all in one go when you do connect.*

4.   Select the **Outbox** folder, Outbox [1], from the **Folders List**. Any messages waiting to be sent are shown here.

Note: *If your **Outbox** is empty (and no number is shown after the folder name on the **Folders List**), then your message has already been sent.*

Exercise 9 - Continued

Note: *The* **Send/Receive All Folders** *button can be used to force* Outlook *to send any waiting messages (if this does not occur automatically).*

5.   Display the **SEND / RECEIVE** tab on the **Ribbon**.

6.   Then, click the **Send/Receive All Folders** button. A progress dialog box, as shown below, may appear for a moment. If you are prompted to connect to the Internet, please do so.

Note: *As it is used frequently, a* **Send/Receive All Folders** *button is also available on the* **Quick Access Toolbar**, . *You can also use the keyboard shortcut <***F9***>.*

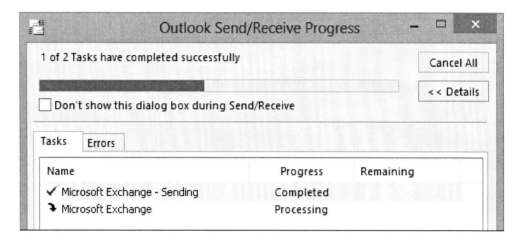

Note: *A* **SEND/RECEIVE** *status message may be shown on the* **Status Bar**. *Always wait for the* **Send/Receive** *process to finish before moving on.*

7.   Select the **Sent Items** folder on the **Folders List**. Notice that a copy of your message is saved here.

8.   If it is not already selected, click the **My First Message** item on the **Message List**. A preview of the message's content appears in the **Reading Pane**.

9.   Leave *Outlook* open for next exercise.

Exercise 10 - Receiving a Message

Guidelines:

When you receive an e-mail it is downloaded and stored in your **Inbox** folder. New and unread messages are shown in the **Message List** in bold, blue type. Once you read the message, its text changes to regular, black type.

Note: *E-mail messages are stored on a mail server (either in your company or at your ISP) which is where they remain until you download them. You do not need to keep the program running all of the time.*

Actions:

1. Select your **Inbox** folder, [Inbox], from the **Folders List**. The folder's contents are shown in the **Message List**.

2. You will receive the message that you sent to your own address in the previous exercise. If it has not appeared in your **Inbox** yet, use the **Send/Receive All Folders** button to check for new messages.

Note: Outlook *will regularly check for new messages automatically, but clicking the **Send/Receive All Folders** button forces it to check for new messages immediately. Bear in mind that it sometimes takes a little while for messages to "pass through the system".*

3. The name on the message indicates who the e-mail was sent **FROM**, followed by the **SUBJECT** and date/time **RECEIVED**. A short, single line *preview* of the message's content will also appear.

Note: *It is possible that Outlook will identify your message as **Junk Mail** and store it in a special **Junk E-mail** folder (if present). If so, open the **Junk E-mail** folder from the **Folders List** on the **Folder Pane** and select the **My First Message** e-mail. Display the **HOME** tab on the **Ribbon** and click the **Junk** button in the **Delete** group. From the submenu that appears, select **Not Junk**. The message will be moved back to the **Inbox**.*

Note: *Notice the **All** and **Unread** filter buttons above the **Message List**. **All** shows all messages in your **Inbox**; **Unread** shows only unread messages. Throughout this guide it is assumed that **All** is always selected.*

4. Click the **My First Message** e-mail once on the **Message List**, if it is not already selected, to preview its contents in the **Reading Pane**.

Exercise 10 - Continued

5. Double click the **My First Message** e-mail on the **Message List** to open it in a new window. Notice the features available on the **Ribbon**.

6. Close the e-mail by clicking the **Close** button, ☒, found towards the top right corner of the message window.

7. Notice the **My First Message** e-mail on the **Message List**. As the message is now considered to have been read (as you have opened it), it will appear with regular black type.

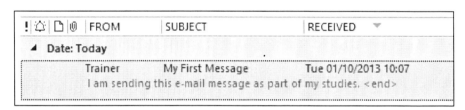

Note: *Sometimes you will open an e-mail but not have time to read it. Being able to mark items as* ***Unread*** *so that you can return to and read them later is a very useful feature.*

8. To mark the **My First Message** e-mail as **Unread**, first make sure the **HOME** tab is displayed.

9. Then, click the **Unread/Read** button in the **Tags** group. The text reverts to bold, blue formatting. This is how all unread e-mail messages are formatted.

Note: *Similarly, you can use the* ***Unread/Read*** *button to mark an unread message as read.*

Note: *Notice the number shown in brackets after the folder name; if shown, this indicates the number of* <u>unread</u> *messages in that folder.*

10. Click the **Unread/Read** button again to mark the message as read again.

11. Close *Outlook*.

Exercise 11 - Revision

Guidelines:

At the end of every section you get the chance to complete one or more revision exercises to develop your skills. You should aim to complete the following steps without referring back to the previous exercises.

Actions:

1.   Open Outlook.

2.   Create a new e-mail message with the subject: **Developing My Skills**.

3.   Enter your own e-mail address in the **To** box.

4.   In the **Message Area** type:

      I must remember to check my e-mail regularly!

5.   Send the message.

6.   Check your **Outbox** to make sure that the new e-mail has been sent (use the **Send/Receive All Folders** button if necessary on the **SEND / RECEIVE** tab).

7.   View your **Sent Items** folder to check that a copy of the message has been saved.

8.   Return to your **Inbox** and wait for the **Developing My Skills** e-mail to appear (use the **Send/Receive All Folders** button to check for new messages if needed).

9.   Select the new message to preview it in the **Reading Pane**.

10.   Double-click the message to open it in a new window.

11.   Close the **Developing My Skills** message window.

12.   Mark the **Developing My Skills** message as **Unread**.

13.   Mark the **Developing My Skills** message as **Read** again.

14.   Close *Outlook*.

Section 3

Reply & Forward

By the end of this section you should be able to:

Send an E-mail to Multiple Recipients

Reply to an E-mail

Forward an E-mail

Use Automatic Replies

Exercise 12 - Multiple Recipients

Guidelines:

You can easily send any e-mail message that you create to more than one person so that you can communicate with multiple recipients at the same time. Simply enter each person's e-mail address in the **To** box.

If you would like other people to receive a <u>copy</u> of a message, their e-mail addresses can be entered in the **Cc** box (which stands for **Carbon copy**). Typically, recipients of carbon copies are not regarded as participants in a conversation but as observers. For example, if you send an important e-mail to a customer, you could also send a carbon copy to your manager to inform them of your actions.

Note: *The e-mail addresses of people in the* **To** *and* **Cc** *boxes are visible to* all *recipients of a message. To prevent these recipients seeing an address, simply enter it in the* **Bcc** *(**Blind carbon copy**) box instead.*

Actions:

1. Open *Outlook* and start a new e-mail message. In this exercise you will practise sending messages to multiple recipients.

2. Enter your <u>own</u> e-mail address in the **To** box so that you can observe the results of sending this e-mail.

Note: *The semicolon character* ***;*** *is used to separate multiple e-mail addresses. When you click away from the* **To** *or* **Cc** *boxes,* Outlook *will automatically underline each address to show they are valid.*

3. After your own e-mail address, press the semicolon key <;> and then type the address of a second recipient, *Julie*:

julie@bigplanetsupport.co.uk

Note: *A number of* Big Planet Support *e-mail addresses have been created to accompany this guide. They are not monitored by a real person and any message sent to them will be deleted automatically.*

4. You would like to send a *copy* of this message to your manager, **Atesh**. In the **Cc** box, enter his e-mail address:

atesh@bigplanetsupport.co.uk

5. Finally, you would like to send a fourth copy of this message to another recipient, *Fiona*, without any of the other recipients knowing about it. However, notice that there is not a **Bcc** box.

Exercise 12 - Continued

Note: *The **Bcc** box is not visible by default. It can be activated by toggling the **Bcc** button in the **Show Fields** group of the **OPTIONS** tab.*

6. Display the **OPTIONS** tab and click the **Bcc** button in the **Show Fields** group. The **Bcc** box appears below the **Cc** box.

7. In the **Bcc** box, enter *Fiona's* e-mail address:

fiona@bigplanetsupport.co.uk

8. Enter the subject: **Tomorrow's Meeting**.

9. In the **Message Area**, type the following text:

Don't forget the meeting with the area manager at 2pm tomorrow.

10. Send the message. After a moment you will receive the e-mail back in your **Inbox** folder (use the **Send/Receive All Folders** button if needed).

11. Select the e-mail in the **Message List** to preview it in the **Reading Pane**.

Note: *The recipients Julie, Atesh, Fiona and you will all receive the e-mail. Notice that you can see the addresses of everyone that the message was addressed to, apart from Fiona who received a blind carbon copy. Each recipient can also see this list which you need to consider when sending messages to others.*

Note: *If a recipient's name is known to Outlook (because you have already replied to an e-mail from that person or added them to your **People** list), their e-mail address may be replaced by their name. You will learn more about this later.*

Exercise 13 - Replying

Guidelines:

When you receive an e-mail message, it is very easy to create and send a **reply**. A message window will appear where your **reply** can be entered (the original message will be included underneath for reference).

Actions:

1. With the **Tomorrow's Meeting** e-mail selected in your **Inbox** folder, locate and examine the buttons in the **Respond** group.

Note: *The **Reply** button is used to reply to the original sender of an e-mail. The **Reply All** button, however, is used to reply to the original sender and <u>all</u> of the message's original recipients.*

2. First, click the **Reply** button. A new message, addressed only to the sender of the original message (you), will appear in the **Reading Pane**.

Note: *You can reply to or forward a message using Outlook 2013's new inline editing pane (that appears temporarily in the **Reading Pane**), or you can "pop out" the message to open it in a new window.*

3. Click **Pop Out**, Pop Out, just above the **Send** button, to open the message in its own window.

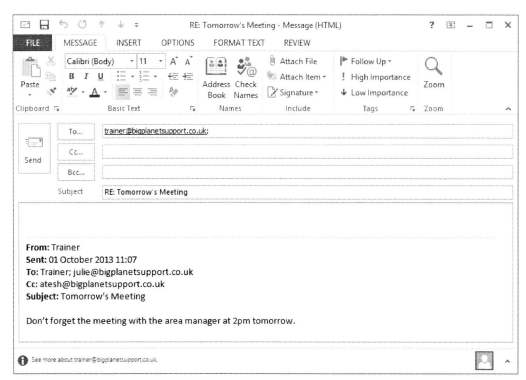

Note: *The **Subject** begins with **RE:** indicating a reply to a previous message.*

Exercise 13 - Continued

4. Enter the following text in the **Message Area** (above the original text):

    Thank you for your message. I have made a note of the details.

Note: *The text of the original message is displayed below your reply. This provides a history of a conversation and allows you to refer back to earlier messages.*

Note: *The reply text appears in a different colour (usually blue) to distinguish it from the original message's text.*

5. Click **Send** to send the message.

6. The **Tomorrow's Meeting** message should still be selected in the **Message List**. Notice the **Information Bar** which shows that you have now replied to it.

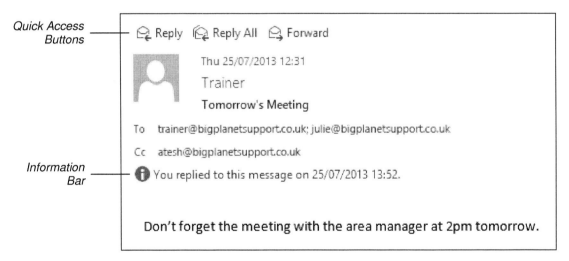

7. Locate the useful **Quick Access Buttons** above the message in the **Reading Pane**. Click the **Reply All** button to create a reply using *Outlook's* inline editing pane.

8. Notice that the original sender and all of the original recipients will now receive a copy of your reply. Click **Discard** to close the reply without sending.

9. When you receive the reply sent in step 5 (which was again addressed to you), select the message in the **Message List** to preview it.

10. Leave *Outlook* open for the next exercise.

Exercise 14 - Forwarding

Guidelines:

A message that you receive can also be **forwarded** to another person. This is useful when you want to send a copy of a message to somebody else that wasn't on the original recipient list.

Note: In business, always consider data protection and only forward messages containing sensitive information to authorised people.

Actions:

1. The **RE: Tomorrow's Meeting** reply should still be selected in the **Message List** (if it is not, select it now).

2. You would like to send this message to another person. Click the **Forward** button in the **Respond** group.

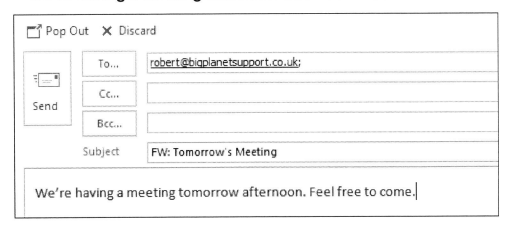

*Note: Notice that the **Subject** now begins with **FW:** indicating a forwarded message. You are always free to change the **Subject** text if needed.*

3. Using *Outlook's* inline editing pane, enter the e-mail address **robert@bigplanetsupport.co.uk** in the **To** box.

4. An additional message can be included above the original e-mail text. In the **Message Area**, enter the following (above the original text):

    We're having a meeting tomorrow afternoon. Feel free to come.

5. Send the e-mail. The message has been forwarded.

Exercise 15 - Automatic Replies

Guidelines:

Most e-mail programs and web-based e-mail services feature the ability to send automatic responses to incoming messages. This is useful when you are on holiday or out of the office for a long period of time.

In *Outlook*, this feature is traditionally called the **Out of Office Assistant** and works even when the program is not running.

Note: *The **Out of Office Assistant** is only available if your mail server or ISP supports it.*

Actions:

1. Click the **FILE** tab and, with **Info** selected, examine the options that appear on the screen.

2. Locate the **Automatic Replies** button, if present, and read the short description of this useful feature.

Note: *If the **Automatic Replies** button is not available, you cannot use the **Out of Office Assistant**. Simply read the remainder of this exercise for information.*

3. Click the **Automatic Replies** button and examine the **Automatic Replies** dialog box that appears.

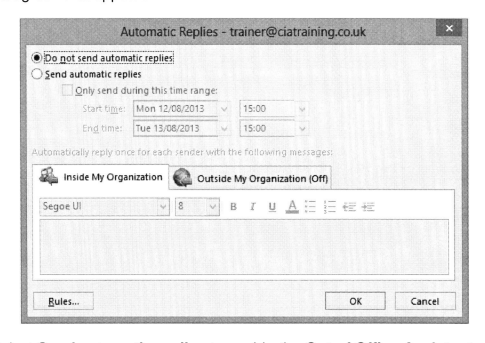

4. Select **Send automatic replies** to enable the **Out of Office Assistant**.

Note: *You can restrict auto-replies to specific dates and times. To do this, select **Only send during this time range** and choose a **Start time** and **End time**.*

Exercise 15 - Continued

Note: Outlook *is able to determine if an incoming e-mail is from a colleague in your organisation or not. You can send different replies depending on the type of person sending the message.*

5.   With the **Inside My Organization** tab selected, enter a short reply to your colleagues in the **Message Area** (as the example below demonstrates).

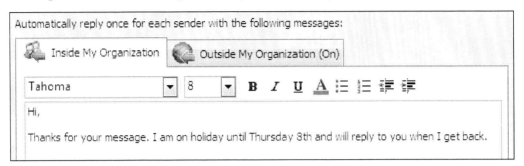

6.   Select the **Outside My Organization** tab and enter another short reply in the **Message Area** (as the example below demonstrates).

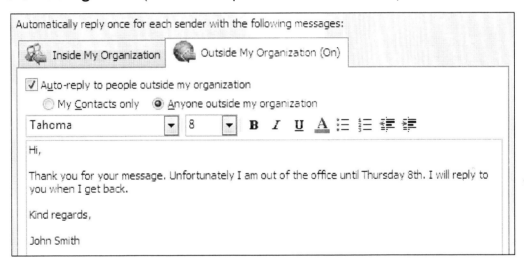

Note: It is recommended that you use a formal, professional tone in your replies.

7.   Click **OK**. The **Automatic Replies** feature is now enabled and all incoming e-mail will receive an automatic reply.

8.   Click **Turn off** to disable the **Automatic Replies** feature. *Outlook* will no longer send automatic replies.

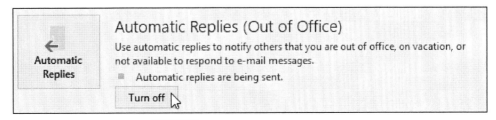

9.   Click the **Back** button, [←], to return to **Mail** view.

Exercise 16 - Revision

Guidelines:

At the end of every section you get the chance to complete one or more revision exercises to develop your skills. You should aim to complete the following steps without referring back to the previous exercises.

Actions:

1. Create a new, <u>self-addressed</u> e-mail message.

2. Make sure a **Carbon copy** will go to **julie@bigplanetsupport.co.uk**.

3. Include a **Blind carbon copy** to **john@bigplanetsupport.co.uk**.

4. What is the difference between a carbon copy and blind carbon copy?

5. Enter the subject **Grand Opening Party**. Then enter the following text in the **Message Area**:

    To celebrate the grand opening of the new Rumbling Bellies restaurant, you are invited to a party next Friday at 6pm.

6. Send the e-mail and wait for it to return (as it was addressed to you).

Note: *Don't forget to use the **Send/Receive All Folders** button to check for new messages.*

7. Preview the **Grand Opening Party** message in the **Reading Pane**.

8. Reply to the **Grand Opening Party** message, including the following additional text:

    Sounds great! I'll be there.

9. Forward a copy of the same **Grand Opening Party** e-mail to the following address: **robert@bigplanetsupport.co.uk**. Include the message:

    This event sounds like fun. Fancy coming along?

10. Open your **Sent Items** folder and preview the reply and forwarded messages sent in this revision exercise.

11. Return to your **Inbox** folder.

Note: *Sample answers can be found at the back of the guide.*

Section 4

Attachments

By the end of this section you should be able to:

Send File Attachments Using E-mail

Receive Attachments

Save Attachments

Remove Attachments

Understand Attachment Restrictions

Send Zipped Attachments

Exercise 17 - Sending Attachments

Guidelines:

It is possible to **attach** files stored on your computer to an e-mail message. The attached files are then sent along with the message and can be saved or opened by the person who receives it. This makes it easy to send documents, spreadsheets, presentations, publications or pictures anywhere in the world.

Actions:

1. Start a new message and address it to yourself so that you can observe the results of this exercise.

2. Enter the subject as **Candidate**.

3. In the **Message Area**, enter the following text:

    I've had another application for the post of Head Chef. His CV and photograph are attached.

4. **Maximise** the message window and click the **Attach File** button in the **Include** group on the **Ribbon**. The **Insert File** dialog box appears.

5. Navigate to the location where the data files for this guide are stored (see note on page 3). Then, click the **CV** file once to select it.

6. Click the **Insert** button and the document file is attached to the e-mail.

7. Notice that the attachment appears in a new **Attached** box under the **Subject**.

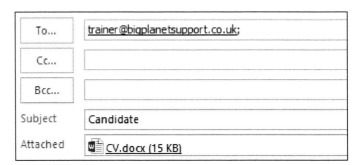

Note: *Depending on your default settings, attachments may appear as icons in the **Message Area** instead.*

8. To add a second attachment, click the **Attach File** button again. This time, attach the image file **John**.

9. Send the message.

Exercise 18 - Receiving Attachments

Guidelines:

When you receive an e-mail containing attachments, it will appear in the **Message List** marked with a paperclip icon, .

Actions:

1. The **Candidate** message sent to your own e-mail address in the previous exercise should now appear in your **Inbox** folder (remember to use the **Send/Receive All Folders** button if necessary).

2. Notice the paperclip icon on the **Message List** – this indicates that the e-mail has attachments.

Attachment icon

3. Select the message to preview it in the **Reading Pane**. The attached files appear as tabs along the top of the message.

Attachment tabs

4. Click the **CV** tab once to preview the attached file in the **Reading Pane**. Notice the new **ATTACHMENTS** tab that has appeared on the **Ribbon**.

Note: *If a security warning appears, click the **Preview file** button. Because of the danger of viruses in e-mail attachments, you should only open or preview messages from trustworthy sources. Even then it is recommended that you save the file to your computer first and scan it with your antivirus software.*

5. Click the attachment **John** to preview the image file.

Note: *You can double-click a tab to open the attachment. Alternatively, click the **Open** button on the **Ribbon**.*

6. Finally, click the **Message** tab to return to the e-mail's message text.

Exercise 19 - Saving Attachments

Guidelines:

E-mail file attachments can be saved to your computer outside of your *Outlook* mailbox structure.

Note: *It is good practice to save trusted file attachments to your computer and scan them with your antivirus software <u>before</u> opening.*

Actions:

1.   The **Candidate** message received in the previous exercise should still be selected in the **Message List**. In this exercise you will save the two attached files to your computer.

2.   Click the **CV** tab once to preview the attached file in the **Reading Pane**. Then, examine the options that appear on the **ATTACHMENTS** tab on the **Ribbon**.

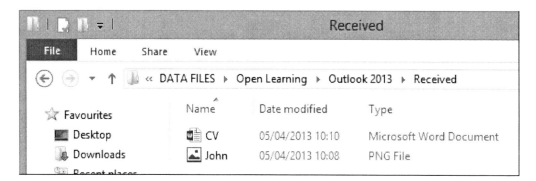

3.   To save the selected attachment to your computer, click **Save As** in the **Actions** group.

4.   The **Save Attachment** dialog box appears. Navigate to the location where the data files for this guide are stored. Then, open the **Received** folder.

5.   Click **Save** to save the attached file.

6.   Using the same technique, preview and then save the **John** attachment to the **Received** data files folder.

Note: *The **Save All Attachments** button can be used to save multiple files at the same time.*

7.   Open *Windows File Explorer* and navigate to the data files folder for this guide. Then, open the **Received** folder to see the saved files.

	Received
File Home Share View	
← → ▾ ↑ « DATA FILES ▸ Open Learning ▸ Outlook 2013 ▸ Received	
	Name	Date modified	Type
☆ Favourites			
■ Desktop	CV	05/04/2013 10:10	Microsoft Word Document
Downloads	John	05/04/2013 10:08	PNG File

Note: *You can now check the files for viruses before opening them.*

8.   Close the **Documents** window and return to *Outlook*.

Exercise 20 - Zipped Attachments

Guidelines:

In practice, it is often a good idea to **zip** multiple files together before attaching them to an e-mail. This gathers them all into one "compressed" package, reducing their overall size and making the message much quicker to send.

Note: *Avoid sending large e-mail attachments as these can cause problems for the recipient. For example, the files could exceed mailbox size limits or take too long to download. As a guide, anything more than 5Mb is probably too large.*

Note: *Because of the risk of viruses,* Outlook *will generally block unsafe file attachments. These include executable files and* Access *databases. However, zipping them up first will usually allow you to send them.*

Actions:

1.   Display the **HOME** tab and start a new e-mail message.

2.   Address it to yourself so that you can observe the results of this exercise.

3.   Enter the subject as **Monthly Meeting**.

4.   In the **Message Area**, enter the following text:

     Find attached Agenda and Staff files for this month's meeting. Please treat this information as private and confidential.

5.   Using the **Attach File** button in the **Include** group on the **Ribbon**, attach the data files **Agenda** and **Staff**. Make a note of the size of the files.

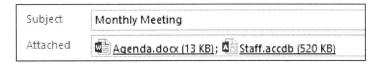

Note: *Due to the file's type, the recipient may have problems with the **Staff** database file.*

6.   You decide it would be better to include a zip of the two files instead. First, the two attachments must be removed from the **Monthly Meeting** e-mail. Select the attachment **Agenda** by clicking it once.

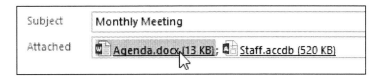

7.   Press <**Delete**> to remove it.

8.   Using the same technique, remove the **Staff** attachment too.

Exercise 20 - Continued

Note: *A zip file containing the* **Agenda** *and* **Staff** *files has already been created for you. This can be found in the data files folder.*

9.   Using the **Attach File** button in the **Include** group, attach the zip file **Meeting Files**.

10. Notice the size of the zip file; it is significantly smaller than the two original files combined.

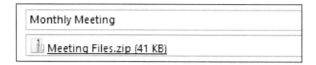

Note: *To work with the contents of a zip file, you can right click on it in* Windows File Explorer *and select* **Extract All**. *Follow the extraction instructions that appear.*

11. Send the message.

Exercise 21 - Revision

Guidelines:

At the end of every section you get the chance to complete one or more revision exercises to develop your skills. You should aim to complete the following steps without referring back to the previous exercises.

Actions:

1. Create an e-mail message addressed to: **julie@bigplanetsupport.co.uk**

2. Enter your own e-mail address in the **Cc** box.

3. Enter the subject **Car Service**.

4. Type the following text in the **Message Area**:

    Remember to book the company car in for a service before the end of this month.

5. You have received a discount voucher from a local garage that you would like to share. Attach the file **Voucher** from the data files.

6. Send the message and wait for your copy to return (don't forget to use the **Send/Receive All Folders** button to check for new messages).

7. Preview the **Car Service** message in the **Reading Pane**. Then, preview the **Voucher** attachment by clicking its tab.

8. Save the **Voucher** attachment to the **Received** data files folder.

9. Return to the **Message** text and leave *Outlook* open.

Section 5

Message Tools

By the end of this section you should be able to:

Set a Message's Importance

Flag a Message

Track a Message

Recall a Message

Use E-mail as a Voting Tool

Open and Close the To-Do Bar

Exercise 22 - Message Importance

Guidelines:

Messages have **Normal** priority by default, but it is possible to change their importance to either **High** or **Low**. This does not mean that they are sent more quickly or slowly, only that the recipient will be aware of their urgency by an icon on the message.

Actions:

1. Start a new message and address it to yourself so that you can observe the results of this exercise.

2. Enter the subject as **Urgent!** and, in the **Message Area**, enter the following text:

    Don't forget your meeting with the area manager at 2pm today.

3. On the **MESSAGE** tab, click **High Importance**, ! High Importance , in the **Tags** group.

Note: *Notice that the button stays highlighted to indicate the message has high priority. Clicking it again will reset the message to normal priority.*

4. Send the e-mail. When the message arrives back in your **Inbox** it will have a **High Importance** icon set, ▯.

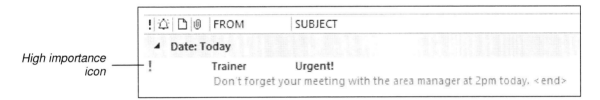

High importance icon ——

5. Select the message in the **Message List** to preview it in the **Reading Pane**. An **Information Banner** appears at the top.

Information Banner ——

Note: *The process to make a message low importance is very similar. Simply click the **Low Importance** button when creating a new message. The message will have a low importance icon when it is received, ⬇.*

6. Leave *Outlook* open for the next exercise.

Exercise 23 - Following Up

Guidelines:

It is possible to **flag** messages in *Outlook* so that you can "follow them up" later. For example, if you receive an e-mail that you are unable to respond to immediately, you can flag it for further attention.

Note: *Additional custom flags can be created for specific types of actions (e.g. make a telephone call, reply to an e-mail, etc.) and can have a start date and a due date. You can also choose to receive a reminder at a future date and time.*

Actions:

1.   With the **Urgent!** e-mail selected in the **Message List**, display the **HOME** tab and click the **Follow Up** button in the **Tags** group.

Note: *Depending on how* Outlook *is set up, you may only see* **Flag Message**.

2.   Examine the **Follow Up** due-dates that are available. From the list that appears, select **Tomorrow**.

Note: *If* **Flag Message** *is the only option available, select that and move to step 12.*

Follow-up flag

3.   Notice that a follow-up flag has now appeared in the **Message List**.

4.   Click the **Follow Up** button in the **Tags** group. From the list that appears, select **Mark Complete**. Observe the effect.

Completed flag

Note: *You can also mark a follow-up flag as complete by simply clicking the flag icon in the* **Message List***.*

Exercise 23 - Continued

5. Click the **Follow Up** button and, this time, select **Next Week**. A new flag is set for this e-mail.

6. To mark this follow-up as complete again, simply click the flag once.

Inactive flag

*Note: Clicking an inactive flag will set a new follow-up flag which is due **Today**.*

7. To clear the flag, click the **Follow Up** button in the **Tags** group. From the list that appears, select **Clear Flag**.

8. To create a custom flag, click the **Follow Up** button in the **Tags** group again and, from the list that appears, select **Custom**.

9. The **Custom** dialog box appears. Display the drop-down list of **Flag to** reasons and select **For Your Information**. Leave the default **Start date** and **Due date** as today.

10. Place a tick in the **Reminder** checkbox and examine the default settings. In the screenshot below, a reminder will appear on-screen at **16:00** on **01/10/2013** (but this will appear differently on your screen).

11. Click **OK**. A flag appears together with a reminder icon, .

Reminder icon

Exercise 23 - Continued

Note: Reminders appear in a pop-up window when Outlook *is running. You can cancel (**Dismiss**) the reminder or delay it (**Snooze**) for a period of time.*

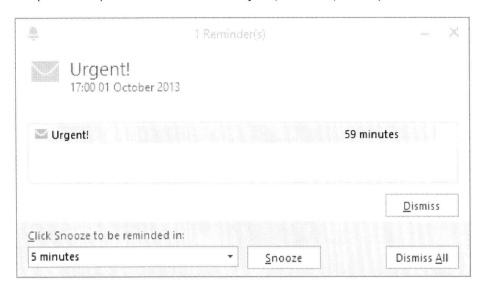

12.   Display the **VIEW** tab and click the **To-Do Bar** button in the **Layout** group. From the options that appear, select **Tasks**.

Note: Flagged messages also appear on the useful Outlook ***To-Do Bar**. This shows upcoming follow-up **tasks**.*

13.   Examine the **To-Do Bar** that appears. In particular, notice that the **Urgent!** e-mail follow-up appears as an outstanding task.

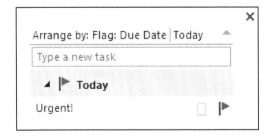

Note: You will learn more about creating and working with tasks in section 10.

14.   Click the **To-Do Bar** button in the **Layout** group and select **Off** to hide the **To-Do Bar** again.

15.   To clear the flag, click the **Follow Up** button in the **Tags** group on the **HOME** tab. From the list that appears, select **Clear Flag**.

*Note: The flag and reminder icon (if one was created) are both removed from the **Message List**.*

16.   Leave *Outlook* open for the next exercise.

Exercise 24 - Message Sensitivity

Guidelines:

If you send an e-mail containing sensitive information, you can mark it as **Personal**, **Private** or **Confidential**. This prompts the recipient to take extra care when dealing with it.

Actions:

1.   Start a new message and address it to yourself so that you can observe the results of this exercise.

2.   Enter the subject as **Employee Appraisal** and type the following text into the **Message Area**:

     Your appraisal for this year is scheduled for next Tuesday.

3.   From the **OPTIONS** tab on the **Ribbon**, click the dialog box launcher located to the right of the **More Options** group title.

4.   The **Properties** dialog box appears.

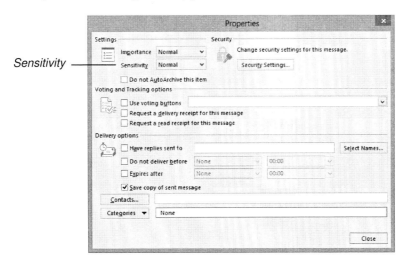

5.   Click the **Sensitivity** drop-down box and examine the options. Select **Confidential**, and then click **Close** to close the dialog box.

6.   Send the message. When you receive it back in your Inbox folder, preview it in the **Reading Pane**. Notice the text on the **Information Bar**.

Exercise 25 - Read Receipts

Guidelines:

To be informed when a recipient reads your e-mail messages, you can request a **Read Receipt**.

Note: *This feature only works if a recipient's e-mail provider supports it. As a result, do not depend on receiving a read receipt.*

Actions:

1. Start a new message and address it to yourself so that you can observe the results of this exercise.

2. Enter the subject as **Wages Query** and type the following text into the **Message Area**:

   I believe there is an error with my wages for this month. Can you look into it for me?

3. From the **OPTIONS** tab on the **Ribbon**, click the checkbox **Request a Read Receipt** in the Tracking group.

Note: *Although used less frequently, you can also request a delivery receipt.*

4. Send the message. When you receive the message back in your **Inbox** folder, double click it in the **Message List** to open it. A read request prompt appears.

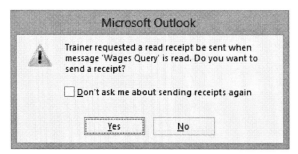

Note: *If no read request prompt appears, your e-mail provider does not support this feature. Please move on to the next exercise.*

5. Click **Yes** to send a read receipt. Read the message and then close it.

6. After a moment you will receive the **Read Receipt** in your **Inbox** (as it was you who sent the original message).

Note: *Use **Read Receipt** requests sparingly as they can quickly become annoying for people to receive and respond to.*

7. Preview the **Read Receipt** in the **Reading Pane**. Notice the **Read Receipt** icon, ✉, in the **Message List**.

Exercise 26 - Recalling Messages

Guidelines:

Once you click the **Send** button it is almost impossible to stop or retreive an e-mail (which is why it is important to check and proof-read your messages before sending them). However, if the recipient's e-mail provider supports it, you can try to recall a message *before* it has been read.

Note: *This feature only works if a recipient's e-mail provider supports it.*

Actions:

1. Start a new message and address it to **julie@bigplanetsupport.co.uk**

2. Enter the subject as **Presentation** and type the following text into the **Message Area**:

    Hi Julie. I am holding a presentation next Thursday in the main training room and you are invited to attend.

3. Click **Send** to send the message.

4. You realise that you have made a mistake: the presentation will be held next *Friday* instead. Let's try to recall and correct the message...

5. Select **Sent Items** in the **Folders List**.

6. Locate and then double-click the recently sent **Presentation** e-mail in the **Message List**.

7. Click the **Actions** button in the **Move** group. Then, from the options that appear, select **Recall This Message**.

Note: *Notice that you can send a request to delete an unread e-mail or replace it with a new message.*

8. Select **Delete unread copies and replace with a new message**.

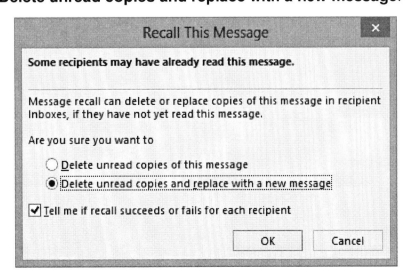

Exercise 26 - Continued

9.   Make sure that **Tell me if recall succeeds or fails for each recipient** box is checked.

10.   Click **OK**. A message window appears in which you can change the original message.

11.   Change **Thursday** in the message to **Friday**.

12.   Click **Send** to send the updated message. Then, close the original message window.

Note: *If the original message has not yet been opened and read, Outlook will try to replace it. If it succeeds, you will receive a **Message Recall Success** message. If not, you will receive a **Message Recall Failure** e-mail (or no reply at all if the recipient's e-mail provider does not support this feature).*

13.   Select your **Inbox** on the **Folders List**.

Note: *It is very difficult to "undo" an e-mail once sent. Check your messages before sending them and never rely on Outlook's recall feature.*

14.   Leave your **Inbox** open for the next exercise.

Exercise 27 - Voting

Guidelines:

A useful feature of *Outlook* is the ability to include **Voting Buttons** in your messages which allow you to easily collect responses to questions or polls.

Note: This feature only works if a recipient's e-mail provider supports it.

Actions:

1.   Start a new message and address it to yourself so that you can observe the results of this exercise.

2.   Enter the subject as **Staff Meeting** and type the following text into the **Message Area**:

I propose we move this week's staff meeting to 2pm. Do you agree? Please vote Yes, No, or Maybe.

3.   From the **OPTIONS** tab on the **Ribbon**, click **Use Voting Buttons** in the **Tracking** group. From the drop-down list that appears, select **Yes; No; Maybe**.

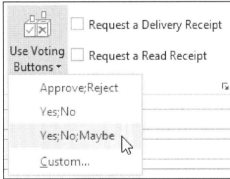

*Note: To create your own voting button labels, click **Custom** and replace the default labels shown with those of your own (separated by semicolons ;).*

4.   Send the message. When you receive it back in your **Inbox** folder, preview it in the **Reading Pane**.

Information Bar ——

Exercise 27 - Continued

Note: *Notice the **Information Bar** at the top of the message, labelled **This message includes voting buttons. Click here to vote.***

5.   Click the **Information Bar** once to display a drop-down list showing available responses.

6.   Click **Yes**. A confirmation prompt appears.

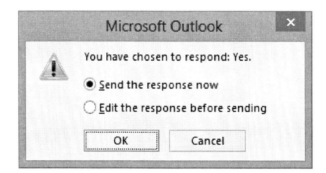

7.   Leave **Send the response now** selected and click **OK** to send your reply.

Note: *Selecting **Edit the response** before sending allows you to add message text to your reply before sending.*

8.   When you receive the reply in your **Inbox** folder, preview the message in the **Reading Pane**.

Note: *Notice the **Information Bar** at the top of the message indicating that the recipient responded **Yes**.*

Note: *To view a summary of responses so far, click the **Information Bar** and select **View voting responses**. Total replies are shown in addition to respondent names. This information is attached to the original e-mail message and stored in **Sent Items**.*

9.   Close the message.

Exercise 28 - Revision

Guidelines:

At the end of every section you get the chance to complete one or more revision exercises to develop your skills. You should aim to complete the following steps without referring back to the previous exercises.

Actions:

1. Create a new, self-addressed e-mail message.

2. Enter the subject as **Team Building Trip**.

3. Type the following text in the **Message Area**:

   This month's outing is to a local paintballing range. Please let me know if you are free next Friday.

4. Change the selected message's priority to **High Importance**.

5. Send the message.

6. When the message arrives back in your **Inbox**, notice the **High Importance** icon, ▮.

7. Flag the **Team Building Trip** message for follow-up today.

8. Show the **To-Do Bar** to find the outstanding follow-up task.

9. Turn off the **To-Do Bar**.

10. If **Custom** appears in the **Follow Up** drop-down, create a custom **Follow up** for the **Team Building Trip** e-mail. Set both the **Start date** and **Due date** to next Friday and create a reminder to occur next Thursday at 2pm.

11. Finally, clear the flag for the **Team Building Trip** e-mail.

12. Leave *Outlook* open.

Section 6

Saving & Printing

By the end of this section you should be able to:

Save a Draft Message

Print a Message

Use Print Preview

Adjust Print Settings

Exercise 29 - Drafts

Guidelines:

Unfinished messages can be saved so that they can be completed and sent at a later date. E-mails saved in this way are known as a **Draft** messages and are saved in your **Drafts** folder.

Actions:

1.   Start a new message and address it to yourself so that you can observe the results of this exercise.

2.   Enter the subject as **Meeting**.

3.   In the **Message Area**, enter the following incomplete sentence:

      Are you available for a meeting on

4.   You need to check the date of the meeting. Click the **Save** button, 🖫, on the message's **Quick Access Toolbar**.

Note: *Alternatively, display the **FILE** tab and select **Save**, or simply press <**Ctrl S**>.*

5.   The message is saved in the **Drafts** folder. Close the message by clicking the **Close** button, ☒, on the message window.

6.   Select **Drafts**, Drafts [1], from the **Folders List**. There should be at least one item in the **Message List** – the **Meeting** draft.

Note: *Notice the number shown in brackets after the folder name; if applicable, this shows the number of draft messages in that folder.*

7.   Double click the message in the **Message List** to open it. You can now continue the e-mail.

8.   In the **Message Area**, complete the e-mail text as follows:

      Are you available for a meeting on **Tuesday at 3pm?**

9.   Send the message. The saved message is removed from the **Drafts** folder and will now appear in the **Sent Items** folder.

10.   Select **Inbox** from the **Folders List**. The **Meeting** message should appear (as it was addressed to you).

Note: *Remember to use the **Send/Receive All Folders** button if necessary to check for new messages.*

11.   Leave *Outlook* open for the next exercise.

Exercise 30 - Printing

Guidelines:

You may need to print a message to provide a hard copy for reference. The **Print** screen can be used to do this.

Note: Always consider whether you really need to print an e-mail message. Doing so unnecessarily is a waste of resources.

Actions:

1. Select the **Meeting** message received in the previous exercise. To print this message, display the **FILE** tab and select **Print**.

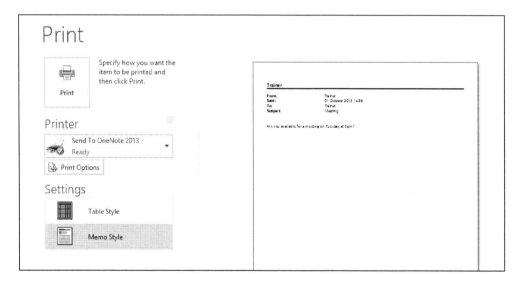

*Note: A **preview** of your message as it will be printed is automatically shown on the preview panel. Clicking the preview will zoom in/out.*

2. Select an *available* printer from the **Printer** drop-down list (your default printer will be automatically selected).

Note: In a work or education environment, you may have access to many printers. Try to find and use the one closest to you. In some situations you may also be charged for printing.

3. Select **Memo Style** under **Settings** (if it is not already selected).

*Note: **Table Style** prints a list of all the items in your **Message List**.*

4. Click the **Print** button to print a single copy of the **Meeting** e-mail on the selected printer. You will automatically return to **Mail** view.

*Note: Alternatively, click the **Back** button, ![back button], to return without printing.*

Exercise 31 - Printing Options

Guidelines:

More print options are available from the **Print** dialog box (e.g. print range, number of copies, etc.).

Actions:

1. With the **Meeting** message still selected in your **Inbox**, display the **FILE** tab and select **Print** again. The *Outlook* **Print** screen is displayed.

*Note: Alternatively press <**Ctrl P**> from **Mail** view.*

2. Click the **Print Options** button, Print Options . The **Print** dialog box appears. Examine the various options available.

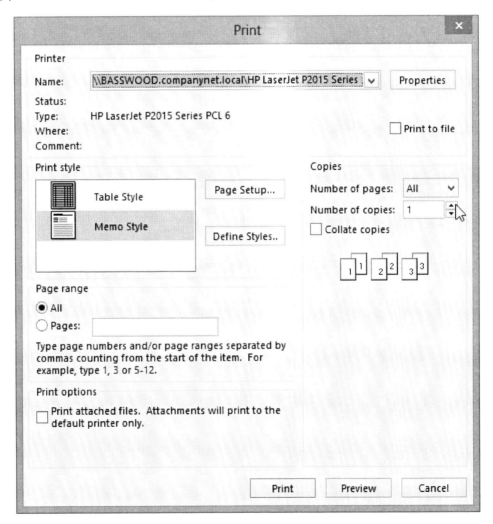

3. Select a printer from the **Printer** drop-down list (your default printer, if available, will be automatically selected again).

Note: Settings specific to the selected printer can be found by clicking **Properties**. *Options usually include colour and print quality.*

Exercise 31 - Continued

4. To print the selected **Meeting** message only, make sure **Memo Style** is selected under **Print style**.

Note: *It is easy to print more than one copy of an e-mail. Simply increase the value in the **Number of copies** box.*

5. Under **Copies**, use the up spinner button to increase the **Number of copies** to **2**. This will print two identical copies of the **Meeting** message.

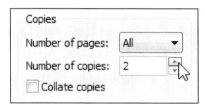

Note: *To print specific pages rather than an entire message, enter the page numbers (or range of page numbers, e.g. 2-3) in the **Pages** box under **Page range**.*

Note: *You can also choose to print all attached files in addition to the message. To do this, select **Print attached files** under **Print options**.*

Note: *Page size, margins and header/footer text can be changed by clicking **Page Setup**. However, it is recommended that you use Outlook's default settings.*

6. Click the **Print** button to print two copies of the **Meeting** message (or click **Cancel** and then the **Back** button to return *without* printing).

7. You will return to the **Mail** view. Leave this open for the next exercise.

Exercise 32 - Revision

Guidelines:

At the end of every section you get the chance to complete one or more revision exercises to develop your skills. You should aim to complete the following steps without referring back to the previous exercises.

Actions:

1. Create a new, self-addressed e-mail message.

2. Enter the subject as **New Computer**.

3. Type the following incomplete message into the **Message Area**:

    Hi,

    The new computer that you requested is now ready to collect

    Thanks.

4. Save the unsent e-mail as a draft and then close the message.

5. Display your **Drafts** folder and resume editing the **New Computer** message. Complete the message text as follows:

    The new computer that you requested is now ready to collect **from head office. Could you please pick it up before 5pm?**

6. Send the message. Check that the sent message has now been removed from your **Drafts** folder.

7. Return to the **Inbox** folder. When the **New Computer** message returns, select it in the **Message List**.

8. Open the **Print** screen and examine the preview that appears. Zoom in to see how the page will look when printed.

9. Select an available printer from the **Printer** drop-down box.

10. Using **Print Options**, print two copies of the **New Computer** message using **Memo Style** (or click **Cancel** and then the **Back** button to return *without* printing).

Section 7

Good Practice

By the end of this section you should be able to:

Copy and Paste Text into a Message

Check a Message's Spelling

Create and Use a Signature

Recognise Good Practice

Send Professional E-mail Messages

Exercise 33 - Copy and Paste Text

Guidelines:

To avoid having to re-type text that already exists elsewhere, it is possible to copy and paste it into an e-mail message.

Note: *In this exercise you will copy text from a document into an e-mail message. In practice, you can copy text from any compatible application.*

Actions:

1. Start a new message and address it to yourself. Enter the subject text as **Company Policy**.

2. Type the following into the **Message Area**:

    Dear Mr. Jones,

    Thank you for your telephone call today. In response to your query, please find below our company's customer service policy.

3. Press <**Enter**> to start a new paragraph.

4. Using *Windows File Explorer*, open your **Documents** and navigate to the data files folder for this guide.

Note: *If you followed the instructions on page 3 correctly, the data files should be installed in the following location on your computer: **Documents\DATA FILES\ Open Learning\Outlook 2013**.*

5. Locate and double-click the document **Policy**. The file will open in your default word processing application (usually *WordPad* or *Microsoft Word*).

6. Select all of the text in the document.

    We always aim to treat our customers with respect and courtesy. We strive to provide a professional and efficient service and respond to enquiries promptly (usually no longer than two days). If a delay occurs, we will politely advise the customer and take action to resolve the problem.

7. Then, click the **Copy** button, 🖺, to copy the text to the *Windows* **Clipboard**.

Note: *Alternatively, press <**Ctrl C**> to copy the selected text.*

8. Close the word processing program without saving changes (if prompted).

9. Then, close the **Documents** window showing this guide's data files, returning to the incomplete **Company Policy** message.

Exercise 33 - Continued

Thank you for your telephone call today. In response to your query, ple
|

10. With the cursor flashing on the empty line at the bottom of the message, click the **Paste** button to paste the copied text (click the button's icon, not its drop-down arrow).

Note: *Alternatively, press <**Ctrl V**>.*

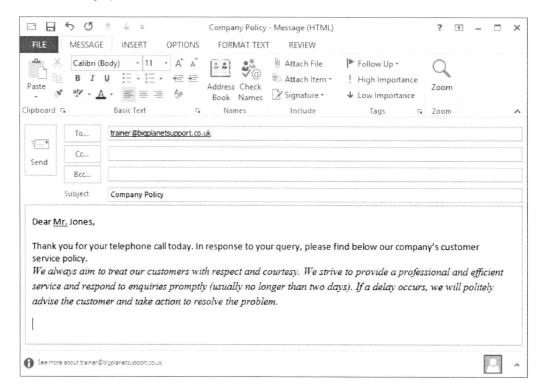

Note: *Notice that the original document's text formatting has been preserved. If needed, the **Paste** button's drop-down arrow can be used to paste plain text* <u>without</u> *formatting.*

11. Click **Send** to send the message.

Note: *Rather than copy large amounts of text into an e-mail message, it is often more appropriate to attach it as a file.*

12. Leave *Outlook* open for the next exercise.

Exercise 34 - Spell Checking

Guidelines:

Outlook contains a spell-checking feature which can be used to check the spelling of new e-mail messages. The spell checker is very similar to the one available in *Microsoft Word*.

Note: *Before you send any e-mail messages, you should always use* Outlook's *spell checking feature to check for errors.*

Actions:

1.   Start a new message and address it to yourself.

2.   Enter the subject text as **Spelling**.

3.   Open your **Documents** and navigate to the data files folder for this guide.

4.   Locate and open the document **Misteaks**.

5.   Ignoring the spelling mistakes for now, copy all of the document's text.

6.   Then, close the word processing program and **Documents** window.

7.   Paste the copied text into the **Spelling** e-mail's **Message Area**.

8.   To correct the spelling in this message, display the **REVIEW** tab and click **Spelling & Grammar** in the **Proofing** group.

9.   The **Spelling and Grammar** dialog box appears, highlighting the first word that the spell checker does not recognise, i.e. "wunder".

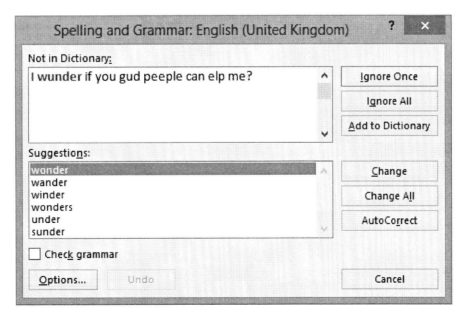

Note: *If a spelling mistake is found, you can choose to **Ignore Once/All** or **Change** the selected word to one of the **Suggestions** given.*

Exercise 34 - Continued

Note: *You can also check for grammar errors by selecting the **Check grammar** box.*

10.   Select the correct choice from the **Suggestions** list (**wonder**) – if it is not already selected – and click **Change**.

11.   The word is changed in the message and the spell checker moves on to the next mistake, i.e. "gud".

12.   Continue to correct the remaining errors as they are found, either by changing or ignoring them.

Note: *The spell checker will also find duplicated words. If any are found, click the **Delete** button in the dialog box to remove one of the duplications.*

13.   When a message appears informing you that the spelling check is complete, click **OK** to close it.

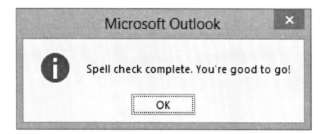

Note: *In general, the spell checker only highlights as spelling mistakes words that are not in its dictionary. For example, the words weak and allot are both incorrect in our example, but because they are valid words, they may not be marked as spelling mistakes (but they may be detected as grammar errors).*

Note: *It is good practice to proof read e-mails before you send them.*

14.   The message is now ready to be sent. Click the **Send** button.

15.   Leave *Outlook* open for the next exercise.

Exercise 35 - Signatures

Guidelines:

An e-mail **signature** is a personalised block of text that is added (automatically or manually) to the end of your e-mail messages. It usually contains your name and contact details, saving you the need to repeatedly enter this information every time you create a message.

Actions:

1. To create a new signature, display the **FILE** tab and select **Options**.

2. When the **Outlook Options** dialog box appears, select **Mail** (which appears on the left side of the window). A number of e-mail settings appear on the right.

3. Under **Compose messages**, locate and click the **Signatures** button. The **Signatures and Stationery** dialog box appears.

4. Click the **New** button to start a new signature. When prompted to enter a name, enter **My Signature**.

5. Click **OK**. A new, blank signature is created. For demonstration purposes, enter the following lines of text into the **Edit signature** box:

   > **John Smith**
   > **IT Training Officer**
   > **Big Planet Support Centre**
   > **Learnersville, LV1 1BP**
   > **trainer@bigplanetsupport.co.uk**
   > **0770 0900 747**

Note: To create a professional signature, try to use the same font type, size and colour throughout. Be sure to include all of your contact details including your job title (if applicable) and make sure there are no spelling mistakes. Avoid using fancy handwriting-style fonts or too many colours.

6. Select all of the signature text and, from the font drop-down box, select **Arial**. From the font size drop-down list, select **10**.

7. Then, select the first line only (**John Smith**) and make the text **Bold** and **Italic**.

   > *John Smith*
   > IT Training Officer
   > Big Planet Support Centre
   > Learnersville, LV1 1BP
   > trainer@bigplanetsupport.co.uk
   > 0770 0900 747

8. Click **OK** and then **OK** again to close the **Outlook Options** window.

Exercise 35 - Continued

9. Start a new message and address it to yourself. Notice that the new signature appears automatically in the **Message Area**, which it now will for all new e-mail messages.

10. Enter the subject text as **Maintenance** and, above the signature, enter the following text:

    Hi,

    Just to let you know that the company's servers will be down for maintenance tonight between 9pm and 10pm.

    Thanks,

11. Your message should now appear as shown below.

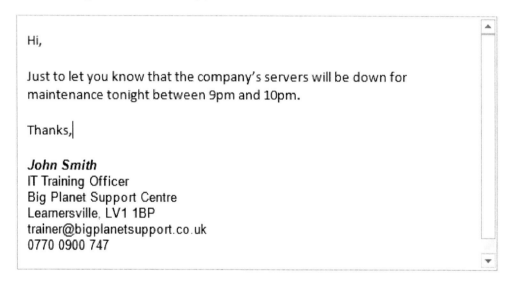

12. Click the **Signature** drop-down button in the **Include** group. Notice that **My Signature** appears.

*Note: You can create more than one signature; each appears in the **Signature** drop-down and can be inserted into the current message by clicking them. It is common to have a personal signature and a business signature for use in different situations.*

13. To delete the new signature, select **Signatures** to display the **Signatures and Stationery** dialog box again.

14. With **My Signature** selected in the **Select signature to edit** box, click **Delete**.

15. Click **Yes** to confirm the deletion and then **OK**. Although your signature has been deleted, it still appears in all messages where it was inserted.

16. Send the message.

Exercise 36 - E-mail Tips

Guidelines:

E-mail is one of the most popular forms of online communication available and is frequently used at home, in education and at work. To help you get the most out of this technology, always consider the following useful tips.

- Keep e-mail to the point and do not forget to add a meaningful subject.

- Do not send e-mails that are likely to offend the person receiving them (including discriminatory or inflammatory information or material).

- Avoid sending large e-mail attachments as these can cause problems for the recipient. As a guideline, anything more than 5Mb is probably too big.

- Use appropriate language and always spell-check your messages (try to avoid overuse of fancy fonts and colours).

- Do not send sensitive information or material (i.e. material that is protected by copyright or data protection).

Note: *Remember that data protection prohibits you from distributing e-mail or e-mail addresses to others without permission.*

- Consider carefully who you "copy in" to e-mails. Respect other people's confidentiality and avoid inappropriate or illegal disclosure of information.

Note: *Be careful using the* **Reply All** *feature. Are you sure you want to include all of the original recipients in your reply?*

- If necessary, use the Blind carbon copy (**Bcc**) feature to hide the e-mail addresses of recipients.

- Do not be distracted by irrelevant messages (especially jokes and junk mail), and do not use work e-mail for personal activities.

- Learn to deal with "e-mail overload". Prioritise messages and respond to urgent requests first.

- When accessing e-mail using a shared computer, always remember to log out when you are finished.

- Remember that e-mail attachments are one of the main sources of viruses. <u>Never</u> open file attachments from people you do not trust.

- If you do need to open an attachment, save it to a *Windows* folder and scan it first using antivirus software.

Exercise 37 - Professional Considerations

Guidelines:

Whether you use e-mail at home, in education or in the workplace, it is likely that the number of messages you receive will grow and grow and grow. On average, research shows that office workers receive over 40 e-mail messages per day – it doesn't take long for your Inbox to fill up with spam, customer enquiries and urgent requests for information.

Deciding when and how to respond to e-mail messages depends on many considerations such as the type of request, the sender, and the urgency of the message. At work, you must learn to prioritise your e-mail responses to meet the requirements of your job and your company's customer service promises.

Indeed, customers expect a timely response to their e-mails. Your company will usually have a policy which states how long customers will need to wait before receiving a response (typically this is within 24 hours or the next working day). Make sure you are aware of these guidelines and try your best to achieve their targets.

Note: *If you believe an e-mail will take a long time to respond to (perhaps because you need to gather information first), simply send a quick but polite reply to the sender informing them of this. It will serve to put their mind at ease and allow you more time to create a response.*

To help you get to grips with managing your Inbox, try these simple tips:

- Send concise messages using a formal style of language (e.g. "you will" rather than "you'll"). Also avoid any unnecessary complexity.

- Address the e-mail appropriately (i.e. "Dear Mr. Smith,") and use a professional signature.

- Gather all information needed to respond to a request before you reply.

- If you need to request further information, ask the right questions and pre-empt any further issues that you or the sender may have.

- Move important e-mails such as customer enquiries and requests for information to the top of your "to-do" list.

Note: Outlook's *follow-up flags are useful for reminding you of important e-mail tasks.*

- If your colleagues need information to answer important enquiries of their own, be sure to respond to them quickly.

- Be careful not to let e-mail negatively impact on your other duties or responsibilities.

Exercise 38 - Revision

Guidelines:

At the end of every section you get the chance to complete one or more revision exercises to develop your skills. You should aim to complete the following steps without referring back to the previous exercises.

Actions:

1. Create a new, informal signature for yourself named **Personal**.

2. Create a new, self-addressed e-mail message. Notice that the **Personal** signature text appears automatically.

3. Enter the subject as **Holiday**.

4. Type the following incomplete message into the **Message Area**:

    Hi,

    I've just heard that you are going on holiday to Colorado and will be visiting the Grand Canyon. Here's something that may interest you:

5. Press <**Enter**> to create a new paragraph.

6. Open your **Documents** and navigate to the data files folder for this guide.

7. Locate and open the document **Colorado**.

8. Ignore the spelling errors and copy all of the document's text.

9. Close the program that opened **Colorado** and then close the **Documents** window.

10. Paste the copied text into the **Holiday** e-mail on the blank line at the bottom of the **Message Area**.

11. Correct the spelling in this message.

12. Delete the **Personal** signature.

13. Send the message.

Section 8

Contacts

By the end of this section you should be able to:

Use Outlook's People Feature

Add and Remove Contacts

Maintain and Edit Contacts

Create a Contact Group

Send Messages to Contacts

Delete Contacts

Exercise 39 - People View

Guidelines:

Over time you will find that many of the e-mail messages that you create will be sent to the same group of people (your "contacts"). Often, these will be friends, family or work colleagues. To avoid having to remember their e-mail addresses and contact details, you can store them as **Contacts** in *Outlook's* **People** view.

Actions:

1. From the bottom of the *Outlook* **Folder Pane**, click the **People** view button.

2. Familiarise yourself with the **People** view that appears.

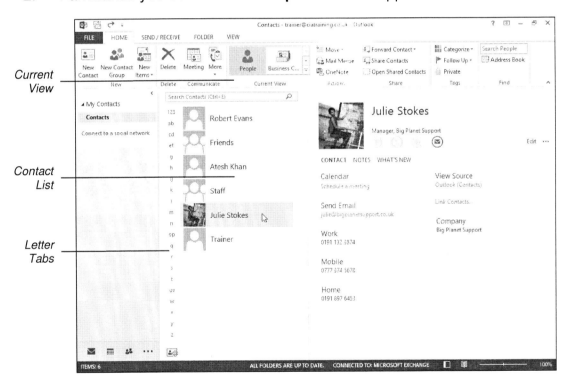

Note: *If you have never used* **People** *view before, it is likely that the* **Contact List** *shown will be empty. In the next exercise you will create new contacts.*

3. Notice the contact display options in the **Current View** group on the **Ribbon**. These allow you to display your contact information in various ways (**People** should be selected).

Note: *The* **Letter Tabs** *displayed vertically down the left side of the* **Contact List** *can help speed up the finding of a contact. Simply click the letter tab that matches your contact's first or second initial.*

Exercise 40 - Adding Contacts

Guidelines:

New **Contacts** can be added to the **People** view by completing a simple form. The information stored can include general details such as name, job title, company name, address, e-mail address, and various phone numbers.

Actions:

1. To create a new contact, click the **New Contact** button in the **New** group on the **HOME** tab.

2. Examine the **Untitled Contact** window that appears.

3. Enter your <u>own</u> personal details into the text boxes. You do not need to complete every box, but make sure you enter your real e-mail address correctly as this will be used in later exercises.

Note: You can use *<Tab>* and *<Shift + Tab>* to move between text boxes.

Note: *If any dialog boxes appear (e.g. prompts to check full name or conversion of telephone numbers), click **Cancel** to continue.*

4. After all of the information has been entered, click the **Save & Close** button in the **Actions** group.

5. Notice the personalised contact that has been created for you.

Note: *Make sure **People** is selected in the **Current View** group on the **Ribbon**.*

6. Let's try adding a few more contacts. Click the **New Contact** button again and enter the details shown on the following page.

Exercise 40 - Continued

Full Name:	**Fiona Jones**
Company:	**Big Planet Support**
Job title:	**Reception Assistant**
E-mail:	**fiona@bigplanetsupport.co.uk**
Business (phone):	**0770 0900 823**

Note: *Always make sure you enter details accurately, especially e-mail addresses and phone numbers.*

Note: *Personal details such as date of birth, nickname or anniversary can also be included by selecting **Details** in the **Show** group.*

7. **Save & Close** the new contact. The new contact is created and added to your **Contact List**.

8. Add the following friend as a new contact:

Full Name:	**Hassan Khan**
Company:	**Big Planet Support**
Job title:	**Custom Contact Officer**
E-mail:	**hassan@bigplanetsupport.co.uk**
Business (phone):	**0770 0900 472**
Mobile (phone):	**0770 0900 526**

9. Examine the new contacts created by selecting them in the **Contact List**. Their details are shown in the **Reading Pane**.

Note: *Notice the **Edit** contact button and **View Source** link in the **Reading Pane**. You will use these in the next exercise to edit a contact's details.*

10. Leave the **People** view open for the next exercise.

Note: *Clicking **Connect to a social network** on the **Folder Pane** allows you to import contacts from your various social networks.*

Exercise 41 - Editing Contacts

Guidelines:

Outlook makes it easy to change contact details by simply double-clicking an entry in **People** view. The record can then be edited as required before selecting **Save & Close** to update the information.

Actions:

1. The **People** view should still be open from the previous exercise. Locate and select the entry for *Fiona Jones* in the **Contact List**.

2. You have been informed that she has been promoted to **Reception Manager** and her work telephone number has changed to **0770 0900 583**. Let's edit her contact record...

3. Click the **Edit** button, $\boxed{\text{Edit} \quad \text{•••}}$, found to the right of the **Reading Pane**.

Note: *Alternatively, double click the entry for* Fiona Jones *in the* **Contact List***.*

4. The **Contact** window appears. Change *Fiona's* job title to **Reception Manager** and her **Business** phone number to **0770 0900 583**.

5. Click **Save** to save the new information and then close the contact editing window. Notice that *Fiona's* information in the **Reading Pane** is updated.

Note: *To add new information to a contact, click the link below* **View Source** *instead.*

6. *Hassan Khan* has transferred to another department. His new job title is **IT Support Executive** and his **Business** phone number is **0770 0900 643**. Change his contact record accordingly.

Exercise 42 - Using Contacts

Guidelines:

The *Outlook* **Address Book** provides another view of your **Contacts**. When you create a new e-mail message (or forward a message to another recipient), it can be used to quickly look up and select e-mail addresses.

Actions:

1. Return to the **Mail** view by clicking the **Mail** view button, 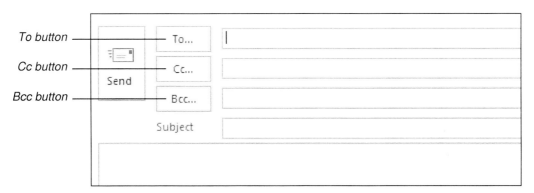, on the *Outlook* **Folder Pane**.

2. Create a new e-mail message by clicking the **New Email** button on the **Ribbon**. An **Untitled Message** window appears.

3. Notice the **To**, **Cc** and **Bcc** buttons. These allow you to open your **Address Book** and select the e-mail addresses of people in your **Contact List**.

4. Click the **To** button, To... . Your **Address Book** opens.

5. From the drop-down box found below **Address Book**, make sure **Contacts** is selected (if it is not already).

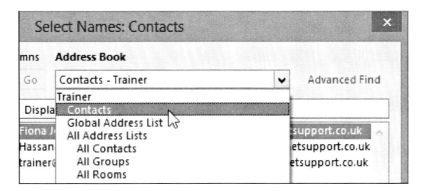

Note: *It is possible to have more than one list of contacts. For example, if your computer is connected to a network (perhaps at work), a **Global Address List** may also be available listing the details and e-mail addresses of all users on the network.*

Exercise 42 - Continued

6. Select the entry for *Fiona Jones* and then click the **To** button, 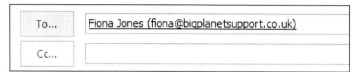. Her e-mail address is copied to the **To** box.

7. Click **OK**. Her e-mail address now also appears in the e-mail's **To** box.

To...	Fiona Jones (fiona@bigplanetsupport.co.uk)
Cc...	

Note: *Notice the format of the contact's name and e-mail address in the **To** field. This is determined by the contents of the **Display as** box when creating a new contact.*

8. Click the **Cc** button, [Cc...]. The **Address Book** appears again.

Note: *Once again, make sure **Contacts** is selected in the **Address Book** drop-down. You will need to check this every time you use your **Address Book**.*

9. Select your <u>own</u> contact record and click the **Cc** button, 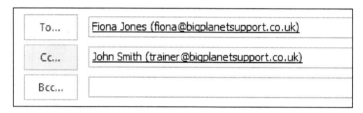. Your e-mail address is copied to the **Cc** box. Click **OK**.

To...	Fiona Jones (fiona@bigplanetsupport.co.uk)
Cc...	John Smith (trainer@bigplanetsupport.co.uk)
Bcc...	

10. Click the **Bcc** button, [Bcc...], and add *Hassan Khan's* e-mail address to the **Bcc** box. Click **OK**.

11. Enter the e-mail message subject as **Your Promotion**.

To...	Fiona Jones (fiona@bigplanetsupport.co.uk)
Cc...	John Smith (trainer@bigplanetsupport.co.uk)
Bcc...	Hassan Khan (hassan@bigplanetsupport.co.uk)
Subject	Your Promotion

12. Finally, enter the following message in the **Message Area**:

Hi Fiona. I hear you have been promoted. Congratulations!

13. Send the message (you should receive a **Carbon copy**).

Note: *When you receive a message from another person, you can add their details to your **Contact List** by right-clicking their name or e-mail address in the **Reading Pane** and selecting **Add to Outlook Contacts**.*

Exercise 43 - Contact Groups

Guidelines:

It is possible to gather individual contacts into **Contact Groups**. A message sent to the group will then be sent to every contact in it.

Note: *A **Contact Group** can also be known as **Address List** or **Distribution List**.*

Actions:

1.   From the *Outlook* **Folder Pane**, click the **People** view button, 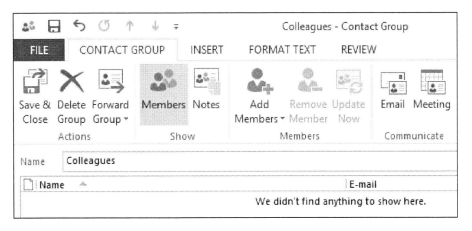.

2.   To create a new **Contact Group**, click the **New Contact Group** button in the **New** group on the **HOME** tab.

Note: *If the **New Contact Group** button is inactive, your mail server or ISP does not support this feature. Move on to Exercise 45.*

3.   Examine the **Untitled Contact Group** window that appears.

4.   The cursor will currently be flashing in the **Name** box. Enter **Colleagues** as the name of this group and press <**Enter**>.

5.   To add contacts to the new group, click the **Add Members** button in the **Members** group. From the submenu that appears, select **From Outlook Contacts**. The **Address Book** appears.

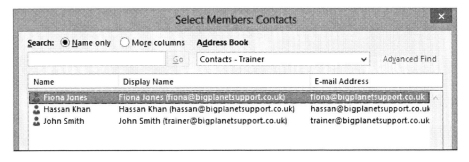

6.   Select *Fiona Jones* from your list of contacts and click the **Members** button. The contact is added to the **Members** box.

Exercise 43 - Continued

7. Using the same technique, add *Hassan Khan*.

8. Click **OK**. The two selected contact records now appear in the **Contact Group**.

9. Click **Save & Close** in the **Actions** group to save the **Contact Group**.

10. Notice that **Colleagues** now appears as a new contact in the **Contact List**. Click the entry once to view this record's information in the **Reading Pane**.

Note: It is easy to add new members to a contact group.

11. Double click the new **Colleagues** group in the **Contact List** to redisplay the **Contact Group** window.

12. To add another contact to the group, click the **Add Members** button and select **From Outlook Contacts**.

13. This time, select your <u>own</u> contact record from your list of contacts and click the **Members** button. The contact is added to the **Members** box.

14. Click **OK**. The three selected contacts now appear in the **Contact Group**.

*Note: To remove a contact, simply select their record and press <**Delete**>. Removing a contact from a **Contact Group** will not remove that person from your **Contact List**.*

15. Click **Save & Close** to update the **Colleagues** group.

Exercise 44 - Using Contact Groups

Guidelines:

Once you have created a **Contact Group**, it appears in your **Address Book** like any other contact. By entering the name of the **Contact Group** in the **To** box of an e-mail, a copy of your message will be sent to every contact contained within it.

Actions:

1.   Return to the **Mail** view by clicking the **Mail** view button, , on the *Outlook* **Folder Pane**.

2.   Start a new e-mail message with the subject **Invitation**. Enter the following text in the **Message Area**:

> **You are invited to a barbecue at my house next Saturday. See you there!**

3.   Click the **To** button to display your **Address Book**. Notice that the **Colleagues** group appears in the list.

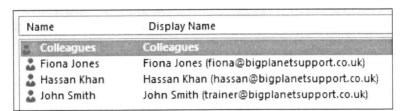

Name	Display Name
Colleagues	Colleagues
Fiona Jones	Fiona Jones (fiona@bigplanetsupport.co.uk)
Hassan Khan	Hassan Khan (hassan@bigplanetsupport.co.uk)
John Smith	John Smith (trainer@bigplanetsupport.co.uk)

*Note: Make sure **Contacts** is selected in the **Address Book** drop-down.*

4.   To send your e-mail message to all of your colleagues in one go, select the **Colleagues** group and then click the **To** button, To -> .

5.   The **Colleagues** group now appears in the **To** box. Click **OK** and notice that the message is now addressed to the **Colleagues** group.

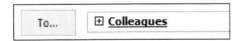

Note: Clicking the expand button, ⊞, will show all contact group members. You can then manually remove recipients if necessary.

6.   Send the message.

7.   All contacts contained within the **Colleagues** group will receive the message (*including you*). Preview it in the **Reading Pane**.

8.   From the *Outlook* **Folder Pane**, click the **People** view button, .

Exercise 45 - Deleting Contacts

Guidelines:

At certain times it may be necessary for you to delete a contact or contact group from your **Contact List**. There are three main techniques available to do this.

Actions:

1. Create and save a new contact for *Julie Stokes* who is **Advertising Manager** at **Big Planet Support**. Her e-mail address is **julie@bigplanetsupport.co.uk**.

2. Select the entry for **Julie Stokes** *in the Contact List*.

3. Click the **Delete** button on the **Ribbon**. The record is removed.

*Note: Once the **Delete** button is clicked, the contact is removed immediately.*

4. From the **Quick Access Toolbar**, click the **Undo Delete** button.

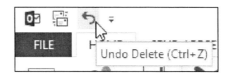

5. The contact details for *Julie Stokes* are restored.

6. This time, *right-click* the entry for **Julie Stokes** in the **Contact List**. From the pop-up menu that appears, select **Delete**.

7. The contact is deleted again. Use the **Quick Access Toolbar** to undo the deletion.

8. Select the entry for **Julie Stokes** in the **Contact List** one last time. Press the <**Delete**> key on your keyboard. The contact is deleted.

Note: As the contact details for Fiona, Hassan and yourself will be used again later in this guide, <u>do not</u> delete these records.

9. Click once to select the entry for the **Colleagues** group.

*Note: The same three **Contact** deletion techniques can be used to remove a group.*

10. Click the **Delete** button on the **Ribbon** and the group is removed.

11. Return to your **Mail** view.

Exercise 46 - People Pane

Guidelines:

The **People Pane** displays information about contacts that you interact with. This includes recent messages, attachments and calendar appointments.

Note: *You can import a list of contacts from a social network. If you do this, the* ***People Pane*** *also allows you to view your contacts' social activity (such as status updates and comments).*

Actions:

1. In **Mail** view, locate and select the **Your Promotion** message that you received in your **Inbox** earlier.

2. Notice the **People Pane** at the bottom of the **Reading Pane**. Small portrait icons will appear for each person involved in the conversation.

Portrait icons

Note: *If you assign a picture to a contact, that picture will appear instead of the default portrait icon.*

3. Place your mouse pointer over a portrait icon to see more details about that person.

Quick contact icons

Note: *Notice the quick contact icons: depending on the contact details recorded for that person (and your device's capabilities), these can be used to quickly start a new conversation using Instant Messaging, telephone, video call or e-mail.*

4. Display the **VIEW** tab and click the **People Pane** button. From the options that appear, select **Normal**. The pane is expanded.

5. Find and select your own portrait icon on the **People Pane**. Then examine the information shown.

6. Notice the activity categories: **WHAT'S NEW**, **MAIL**, **ATTACHMENTS**, etc. Click each in turn and examine the items shown.

Note: *You can select any message shown in this list to open it in a new window.*

7. Click the **People Pane** button again. From the options that appear, select **Minimized**.

Exercise 47 - Revision

Guidelines:

At the end of every section you get the chance to complete one or more revision exercises to develop your skills. You should aim to complete the following steps without referring back to the previous exercises.

Actions:

1. Create and save two new contacts with the following details:

Full Name:	**Atesh Singh**
Company:	**Big Planet Support**
Job title:	**Administrator**
E-mail:	**atesh@bigplanetsupport.co.uk**
Business (phone):	**0770 0900 839**
Home (phone):	**0770 0900 493**

Full Name:	**Robert Evans**
Company:	**Big Planet Support**
Job title:	**Team Leader**
E-mail:	**robert@bigplanetsupport.co.uk**
Business (phone):	**0770 0900 112**
Home (phone):	**0770 0900 730**

2. Create and save a new **Contact Group** called **Staff**.

   Note: *If the **New Contact Group** button is inactive, move on to step 8.*

3. Add *Robert* and *Atesh* to the **Staff** group.

4. Add your <u>own</u> contact record to the **Staff** group.

5. Create and send the following e-mail to the **Staff** group:

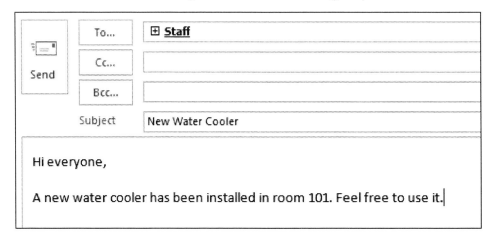

6. Wait for the **New Water Cooler** message to return and examine it in the **Reading Pane**.

Exercise 47 - Continued

7. Delete the **Staff** contact group.

8. *Robert Evan's* home telephone number has changed to: **0770 0900 453**. Update his record accordingly.

9. *Robert Evans* and *Atesh Singh* have moved departments and you will no longer be dealing with them. Delete their contact details.

10. Return to your **Mail** view.

Section 9

Organising E-mail

By the end of this section you should be able to:

Sort Messages in a Folder

Search for Messages

Create Mailbox Folders

Move Messages Between Folders

Create and Delete Rules

Delete and Restore Messages

Permanently Delete Messages

Recognise Junk Mail

Exercise 48 - Sorting Messages

Guidelines:

To help you find messages quickly, you can sort the contents of *any* mailbox folder into order by sender name, received date, subject, and so on.

Note: *Column widths can be adjusted by dragging their boundary bars. Additional headings can also be added by clicking* **Add Columns** *in the* **Arrangement** *group on the* **VIEW** *tab. However, the default headings are ideal for most uses.*

Actions:

1. With your **Inbox** folder selected, notice that information in the **Message List** is grouped into columns. At the top of the screen, column headers are labelled **FROM**, **SUBJECT**, **RECEIVED**, **SIZE**, and so on.

    Column Headers ——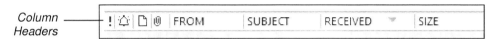

2. By default, e-mail messages in your **Inbox** are shown in the order that they were received, with the newest at the top. This order of sorting is indicated by the small arrow, ⬇, on the **RECEIVED** column header.

3. Click the **RECEIVED** column header once. The arrow turns upside down, indicating that the sort has been reversed. E-mails are now shown in reverse order with the oldest first.

Note: *You can click any of the column headers to sort messages, including the* **Importance**, **Reminder**, **Attachment** *and* **Flag** *header icons. A second click reverses that ordering. This also applies to all other mailbox folders.*

4. Click the **SUBJECT** column header. All e-mail messages are now sorted in alphabetical order by subject.

5. Click the **Subject** column header again to reverse the sort.

6. Click the **Size** column header. All e-mail messages are now sorted in decreasing order of size.

7. Click the **Size** column header again to reverse the sort.

8. Click the **Importance** column header icon, ⬛, to sort all messages by their importance (high importance first).

9. Explore the various other sorts available by selecting each of the column headers on view.

10. When you are finished, click the **RECEIVED** column header once to restore the original sort (newest first).

11. It is easy to add and remove columns in the **Message List**. First, display the **VIEW** tab.

Exercise 48 - Continued

12. Click **Add Columns** in the **Arrangement** group. The **Show Columns** dialog box appears.

13. Examine the columns that can be added in the left-hand **Available columns** box. Scroll down to see the full list.

14. By default, **Frequently-used fields** will be selected in the **Select available columns from** drop-down box. Expand this box and select each of the entries in turn to see more column types.

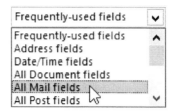

15. When you are finished, select **All Mail fields** from the **Select available columns from** drop-down box.

16. To demonstrate the effect of adding a new column to the **Message List**, find and select **To** under **Available columns**. Then, click the **Add** button to move this column to the bottom of the right-hand box.

Note: *The right-hand box lists the columns shown in the **Message List**. You can use the **Move Up** and **Move Down** buttons to change the order of column headers.*

17. Use the **Move Up** button to move the selected **To** column in the right-hand box between **From** and **Subject**, as shown below.

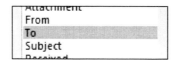

18. Click **OK**. Notice that a **To** column heading now appears at the top of the **Message List** (showing the address that each message was sent to).

19. Click **Add Columns** to display the **Show Columns** dialog box again. Then, select **To** in the right-hand box.

20. Click the **Remove** button to remove this column.

Note: *You can use this technique to remove any of the column headers currently shown in the **Message List**. However, it is recommended that you leave the default column headers as they are for the remainder of this guide.*

21. Click **OK** to confirm the changes and observe the effect – the **To** column is no longer visible.

Exercise 49 - Searching for Messages

Guidelines:

It is possible to search for messages in various ways. For example, you can search for messages sent from a particular person, with a specific subject, or containing certain text.

Actions:

1. With your **Inbox** folder selected, locate the **Search** box (labelled **Search Current Mailbox**) at the top of the **Message List**.

Search Box —

2. Click once in the **Search** box (or press **<Ctrl E>**). Notice that the **SEARCH** tab appears on the **Ribbon**.

3. Type the keyword **meeting** into the **Search** box.

4. As you type, the current folder's **Message List** is "filtered" to display only those messages that match your search criteria.

Note: *By default, keywords can appear in any part of the message, including the sender name, subject or e-mail body.*

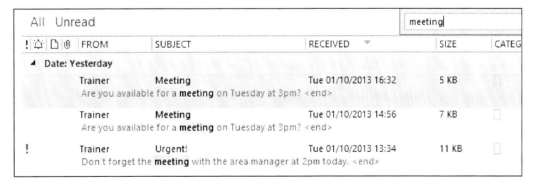

Note: *Depending on the contents of your mailbox and the date items were received, your results may appear differently to that shown above.*

5. Select each message found to preview their contents in the **Reading Pane**. Notice that the keyword is highlighted wherever found.

6. Click the **Close Search** button, ˣ, to the right of the **Search** box, to clear the filter and display all messages again.

7. Click in the **Search** box again (or press **<Ctrl E>**).

Exercise 49 - Continued

8. Examine the various buttons that appear in the **Refine** group on the **SEARCH** tab. These can be used to restrict keyword searches to messages of a specific type (e.g. messages with high priority or messages with attachments).

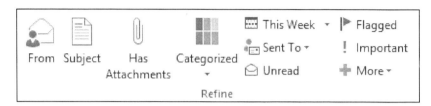

9. Click the **Important** toggle button in the **Refine** group to filter messages with high importance. Examine the **Message List**; a keyword search would now only apply to these types of messages.

10. Click the **Important** button again to clear the filter.

11. Click **Has Attachments** to filter items with an attachment. Examine the **Message List**, and then click the **Has Attachments** button again to clear the filter.

12. Click the **Subject** button in the **Refine** group and type **company**. The text will appear in the **Search** box between brackets.

13. Any message with the keyword **company** in the **Subject** field will now be displayed. Messages with the keyword **company** in the body of the message will <u>not</u> be shown.

Note: *You can search for messages by sender in a similar way by clicking the **From** button in the **Refine** group and entering the person's name.*

Note: *You can use the refine buttons in any order and in any combination.*

14. Feel free to experiment by searching for keywords of your own choosing. Try using the **Refine** buttons to restrict your search to messages from a specific sender or with a specific subject text.

Note: *Outlook may only show recent items in a search. If this occurs, click the **More** button that appears at the bottom of the **Message List**.*

15. Click the **Close Search** button in the **Close** group to clear the search and display all **Inbox** messages again.

Note: *The **Close Search** button has the same effect as clicking the* ˣ *button in the **Search** box.*

Exercise 50 - Creating Mailbox Folders

Guidelines:

It is often a good idea to create a system of subfolders within your **Folders List** to store and organise your e-mail. Messages can then be moved between folders as required.

Actions:

1. Your **Inbox** folder should be open from the previous exercise (if not, select it now from the **Folders List**).

2. To create a new folder in your **Inbox**, display the **FOLDER** tab on the **Ribbon** and click the **New Folder** button.

3. The **Create New Folder** dialog box appears. Notice that the **Inbox** folder is currently selected in the folder list (if it is not, select it now).

4. Enter the name for the new folder as **Training**.

5. Click **OK**. The new folder appears beneath your **Inbox** folder in the **Folders List**, as shown below.

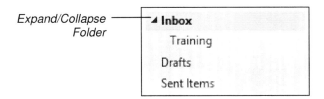

Note: If the **Training** folder is hidden, show it by clicking the **Expand/Collapse** toggle button, ⊿, found to the left of the **Inbox** folder on the **Folders List**.

6. Within the **Message List**, find and select the e-mail **My First Message** that you sent to yourself earlier.

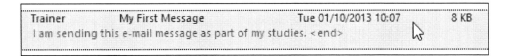

Exercise 50 - Continued

Note: If you cannot find any of the earlier, self-addressed messages mentioned in this exercise, simply read the remaining steps for information.

7.   You are going to move this message to the new **Training** folder. With the **HOME** tab displayed, click the **Move** button within the **Move** group. From the drop-down that appears, select the **Training** folder.

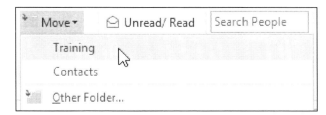

*Note: The **Training** folder may appear anywhere in the list (it will not always be at the top). If the necessary folder does not appear at all, select **Other Folder** and navigate the folders list to find it.*

8.   The message is moved. Select the **Training** folder from the **Folders List** to confirm the move (the contents of the folder will appear in the **Message List**).

9.   Return to the main **Inbox** folder by selecting it from the **Folders List**.

10.   Next, find and select the e-mail with the subject **Candidate** that you sent to yourself earlier.

11.   Click and drag this message from the **Message List** and drop it onto the new **Training** folder. This is a quicker way to move messages between folders.

12.   Open the **Training** folder from the **Folders List** to confirm the move. There should now be two e-mail messages present.

13.   Return to the main **Inbox** folder. Then, using whichever technique you prefer, locate and move the **Monthly Meeting** and **Urgent!** messages to the **Training** folder.

14.   The **Monthly Meeting** message was moved by mistake. Display the **Training** folder and move the message back to the **Inbox** folder.

*Note: Subfolders can be created within any of the folders in the **Folders List**, and messages can be moved freely from folder to folder.*

15.   Return to the main **Inbox** folder.

Exercise 51 - Creating Rules

Guidelines:

Rules can be created in *Outlook* to automatically perform actions when certain messages are received. For example, messages containing specific keywords can be automatically moved to a different folder.

Actions:

1. With your **Inbox** folder open, click the **Rules** button in the **Move** group.

2. From the drop-down that appears, select **Manage Rules & Alerts**. The **Rules and Alerts** dialog box appears.

3. Click **New Rule**, New Rule..., to open the **Rules Wizard**.

Note: The **Rules Wizard** *guides you through the steps needed to create a new rule. You can create rules from scratch, but for this exercise you will use one of the built-in templates (which are sufficient for most needs).*

4. Under **Stay Organised** (**Step 1**), select the rule template **Move messages with specific words in the subject to a folder**.

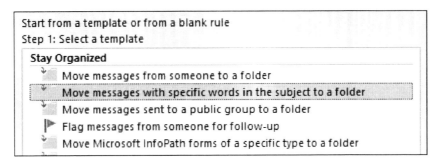

Note: *Familiarise yourself with some of the other templates available.*

5. Notice the rule description that appears in the lower box (**Step 2**). You can customise your new rule here.

6. Click the underlined link **specific words** to customise that step.

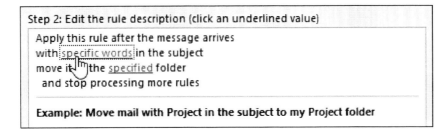

7. You are now prompted to enter specific words to search for in an e-mail's subject. Enter **Open Learning**.

8. Click **Add** to add the words to the **Search list**.

Exercise 51 - Continued

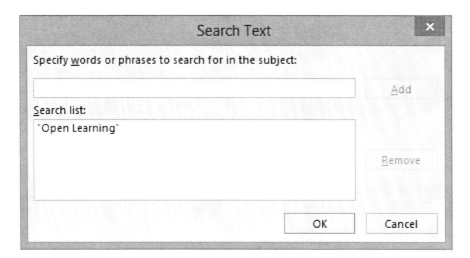

9. Click **OK**. Notice the rule description has been updated.

10. Click the next underlined link, **specified**. Select the folder **Training** from under **Inbox** (you may need to expand the **Inbox** folder).

11. Click **OK**. The rule has been updated again and is now complete.

> Apply this rule after the message arrives
> with Open Learning in the subject
> move it to the Training folder
> and stop processing more rules
>
> ---
>
> **Example: Move mail with Project in the subject to my Project folder**

12. Click **Finish**. Your new rule appears in the **E-mail Rules** list. Click **Apply** to apply the rule, and then **OK** to close the dialog box.

Note: *Your new rule is now active. Any e-mail that you receive with the words **Open Learning** in the subject will now be moved automatically to the **Training** folder.*

13. Create a new e-mail message and address it to yourself.

14. Enter the subject **Open Learning Test Message** and, in the **Message Area**, enter the following text:

    This is a test of my new rule.

15. Send the message. You will receive it back in your **Inbox** in a few moments.

Note: *When the message is returned to you, it will be moved automatically from the **Inbox** folder to the **Training** folder, as per your new rule.*

16. Open the **Training** folder to confirm that the **Open Learning Test Message** e-mail has been automatically moved.

Exercise 52 - Deleting Rules

Guidelines:

Rules can be deleted easily using *Outlook's* **Rules and Alerts** dialog box. Once a rule has been deleted, it will no longer affect your mailbox.

Actions:

1.   Use the **Folders List** to return to your **Inbox**.

2.   To delete the **Open Learning** rule created in the previous exercise (and stop new messages being affected by it) click the **Rules** button on the **Ribbon** and select **Manage Rules & Alerts**.

3.   The **Rules and Alerts** dialog box appears.

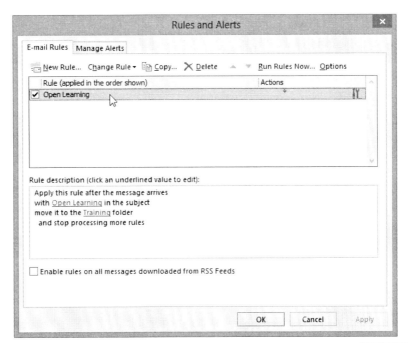

4.   Select the **Open Learning** rule and click the **Delete** button, ✗ Delete.

5.   Click **Yes** to confirm deletion of the rule.

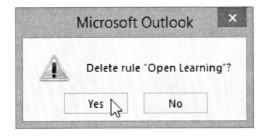

6.   The rule is removed from the list. It will no longer affect any new e-mail messages that you receive.

7.   Click **OK** to close the **Rules and Alerts** dialog box.

Exercise 53 - Phishing and Junk Mail

Guidelines:

Phishing is the process of sending fake e-mail messages in an attempt to steal your identity and gain private information such as user names, passwords and credit card details. If you ever receive an official-looking e-mail asking for this type of information, treat it as a hoax and <u>delete it immediately</u>. This includes any requests from trustworthy organisations to reset login information or verify an account that you didn't personally ask for.

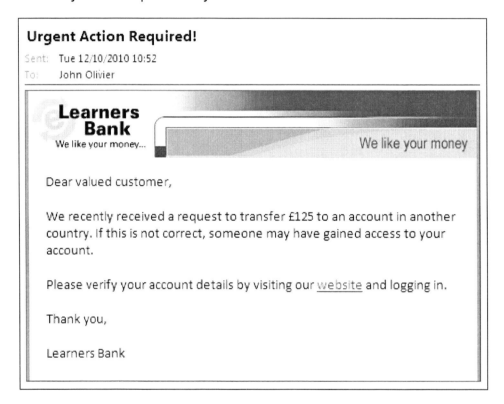

Note: *Businesses will <u>never</u> ask for personal details to be confirmed by e-mail.*

Always ignore any invitation to win prizes, start relationships or make money. Use your common sense: if an offer sounds too good to be true, it usually is!

Note: <u>*Never send money to anyone in response to an e-mail message, no matter how genuine or desperate they may seem.*</u>

Although less of a security risk, junk e-mail can also be a nuisance and can take up a lot of your time. Also known as **spam**, these messages are often used by companies to advertise products. Fortunately, *Outlook* features a **Junk E-mail** filter that will remove obvious spam and scam e-mails from your **Inbox**.

Actions:

1.   Within **Mail** view, select **Junk E-mail** from the **Folders List**.

Note: *If Outlook's **Junk E-mail** filter detects a possible spam message it will be automatically moved into the **Junk E-mail** folder.*

Exercise 53 - Continued

2.　Examine the contents of the **Message List**. Hopefully you have not received any spam and the folder is empty (unlike the example below).

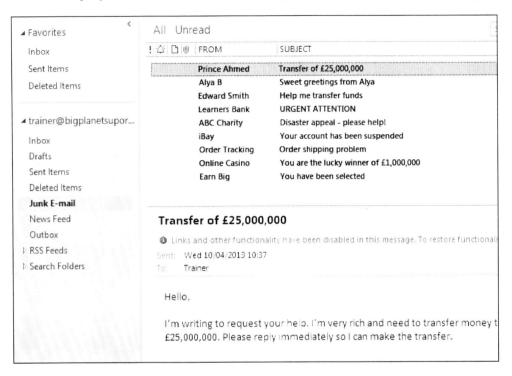

Note:　*As the filter can sometimes get things wrong, it is always worth checking the **Junk E-mail** folder for genuine e-mails that have been removed. Similarly, if a spam e-mail makes it to your **Inbox**, simply delete it.*

3.　With the **HOME** tab displayed, click the **Junk** button, 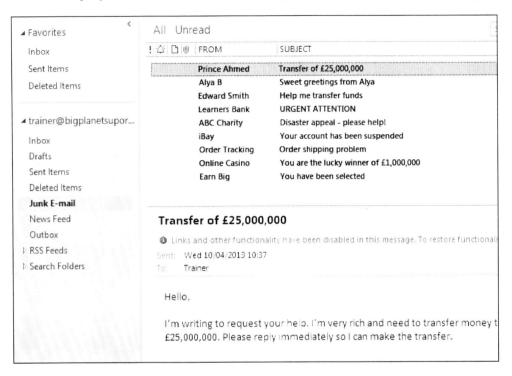, in the **Delete** group. Examine the submenu that appears.

Note:　*If you spot and select a genuine message in your **Junk E-mail** folder, the **Not Junk** option will move it back to the **Inbox**. Alternatively, you can simply drag and drop the message to your **Inbox** folder.*

4.　Select **Junk E-mail Options** and examine the various options that appear. Explore each of the tabs, and then return to **Options**.

Note:　*By default, Outlook's **Junk E-mail** filter removes only the most obvious spam messages from your **Inbox**. If you have problems receiving too much junk, the filter's sensitivity can be increased (at the risk of incorrectly removing a higher amount of genuine e-mail).*

5.　Click the **Safe Senders** tab. Any message sent from the e-mail addresses listed here will always bypass the **Junk E-mail** filter.

6.　Click the **Blocked Senders** tab. Any e-mail received from addresses listed here will be treat as spam and moved straight to **Junk E-mail**.

7.　Click **Cancel** to keep the default, recommended settings.

Exercise 54 - Deleting Messages

Guidelines:

A message that is no longer needed can be deleted from your mailbox. A deleted message will be sent to the **Deleted Items** folder until it is permanently removed (or restored again if you change your mind and want it back).

*Note: Depending on how Outlook is set up, the **Deleted Items** folder may appear with a slightly different name (e.g. **Trash**). If this is the case, you will need to use that folder in place of **Deleted Items**.*

Actions:

1.   Open your **Inbox** folder.

2.   Within the **Message List**, find and select the **Maintenance** e-mail that you sent to yourself earlier.

Note: If you cannot find any of the earlier, self-addressed messages mentioned in this exercise, simply read the steps for information.

3.   To delete this message, click the **Delete** button on the **HOME** tab of the **Ribbon**. The message is moved immediately to the **Deleted Items** folder.

*Note: The **Undo** button, ↶, on the **Quick Access Toolbar** can be used to undo the deletion and restore the message.*

4.   Now, find and select the **Company Policy** message and press the <**Delete**> key on your keyboard to remove it.

5.   Next, find and right-click the **Your Promotion** message and select **Delete** to remove it.

6.   In the **Folders List**, right-click the **Training** subfolder and select **Delete Folder**. Click **Yes** at the prompt to confirm the deletion and remove the folder *and all of its contents*.

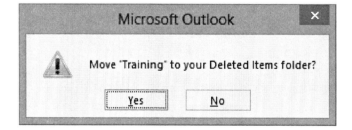

7.   Open the **Deleted Items** folder. Notice that all of the messages deleted in this exercise are shown; you could now restore any item by simply moving it to another folder (using either the **Move** button or via drag and drop).

Note: All deleted Outlook items, including contacts and folders, will also appear.

Exercise 54 - Continued

8. To *permanently* remove all deleted items from the **Deleted Items** folder, display the **FOLDER** tab and click the **Empty Folder** button in the **Clean Up** group.

9. A prompt will appear asking you to confirm the deletion. Click **Yes** (or **No** if you'd rather keep the contents of this folder).

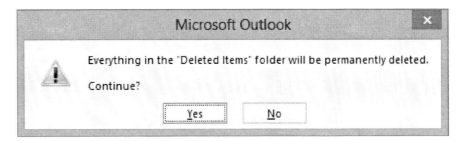

Note: *You can also empty the **Deleted Items** folder by right-clicking it on the* *Folders List and selecting **Empty Folder**.*

10. Similarly, the **Junk E-mail** folder's contents can be deleted. Using any of the techniques described in this exercise, empty the **Junk E-mail** folder.

11. Return to your **Inbox**.

Exercise 55 - Revision

Guidelines:

At the end of every section you get the chance to complete one or more revision exercises to develop your skills. You should aim to complete the following steps without referring back to the previous exercises.

Actions:

1. Create and send a new, self-addressed e-mail with the subject **Holiday Events** and the following message text:

   Do you have any thoughts for potential fund raising events for this summer's holiday period?

2. Organise all messages in your **Inbox** by **Subject** in ascending alphabetical order.

3. Restore ordering by **Received** date (newest messages first).

4. Search for any messages in the **Inbox** containing the keyword **team**.

5. Close the search, then search for any messages with attachments.

6. Close the search, then create a new folder in the **Inbox** called **Revision**.

7. Move the **Holiday Events** message to the **Revision** folder.

8. Create a new rule called **Store after Sending** to move a copy of e-mail messages that you send with **Open Learning** in the subject to the **Revision** folder (hint: start a *blank* rule to check messages *after* sending).

9. Test the new **Store after Sending** rule.

10. If available, delete the **Developing My Skills**, **Grand Opening Party**, **Car Service**, **Team Building Trip**, **New Computer**, **Holiday** and **New Water Cooler** messages.

11. Open the **Revision** folder and delete the **Holiday Events** message.

12. Delete the new **Store after Sending** rule.

13. Return to your **Inbox** folder and delete the **Revision** folder.

14. Move **Holiday Events** from the **Deleted Items** folder back to your **Inbox**.

15. Delete the **Holiday Events** message again.

16. Empty your **Deleted Items** folder (click **No** at the confirmation prompt if you'd rather keep your deleted items).

17. Empty your **Junk E-mail** folder.

Section 10

Tasks & Notes

By the end of this section you should be able to:

Use Task View and Outlook Today

Add a Detailed Task

Mark Tasks as Completed

Assign and Categorise Tasks

Organise and Delete Tasks

Create and Delete Notes

Exercise 56 - Creating Tasks

Guidelines:

Outlook provides a number of tools to help you create "tasks" (jobs and activities that that you would like to track).

Note: *The screenshots provided in this section are for illustrative purposes only. The dates and times selected will appear differently on your screen.*

Actions:

1. Click the **Tasks** view button, 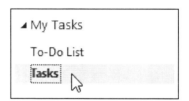, at the bottom of the *Outlook* **Folder Pane**. The **Tasks** view appears.

Note: *If you cannot see the **Tasks** view button, click the **More** button, ⎯⎯⎯, and select **Tasks** from the menu that appears.*

2. A **To-Do List** appears selected by default on the **Folder Pane**.

Note: *The **To-Do List** in **Tasks** view shows all outstanding items in* Outlook, *including tasks, appointments and flagged messages.*

3. To view your **Tasks** list, select **Tasks** on the **Folder Pane** (under **My Tasks**). The screen that appears shows all of your tasks.

> ▲ My Tasks
>
>   To-Do List
>
>   Tasks

Note: ***Tasks** may appear as **Tasks (This computer only)**.*

4. To adjust your screen's layout to match this guide's recommended settings, display the **VIEW** tab and click the **Change View** button. From the options that appear, select **Simple List**.

5. Examine the **Tasks** view and locate the **Task List** and **New Task Box** (labelled **Click here to add a new Task**).

Note: *If this is the first time you have used* Outlook, *the **Task List** will probably be empty.*

Exercise 56 - Continued

6.   You need to call a local ICT supply company to arrange a meeting. So that you don't forget to do this, let's create a new task.

7.   Click once in the **New Task Box** box. Then, type **Call PC Planet**.

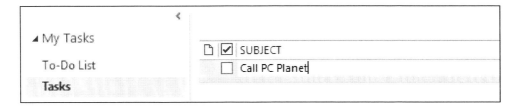

8.   Press <**Enter**>. A new task is created and added to your **Task List**.

9.   The cursor is still flashing in the **New Task Box**. Type **Update Monthly Report** and press <**Enter**> to create a second task.

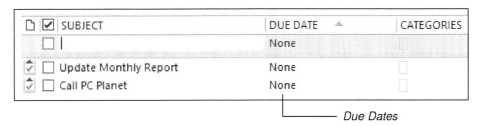

Due Dates

Note: *Tasks do not have a **due date** by default (i.e. a date when a task should be completed by). However, as you will learn in the next exercise, it is easy to add one.*

10.   Notice the column headers at the top of the **Task List**. These are labelled **SUBJECT**, **DUE DATE**, **CATEGORIES**, and so on, and can be used to sort tasks.

Note: *You can click any of the column headers to sort messages. A second click reverses that ordering.*

11.   Make sure tasks are sorted in **DUE DATE** order, as shown below.

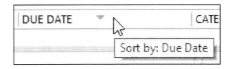

12.   Leave the **Tasks** view open for the next exercise.

Exercise 57 - Creating Detailed Tasks

Guidelines:

The previous exercise introduced a quick and easy way to create a task. However, more detailed tasks can also be created that feature a variety of additional options and settings. For example, you can assign a task a due date, priority, status and reminder.

Actions:

1. Click the **New Task** button in the **New** group on the **HOME** tab. Examine the **Untitled Task** window that appears.

Note: *Double clicking empty space in the **Task List** will also show the **Untitled Task** window.*

2. You are planning to spend some time next week reviewing your training materials. Enter a **Subject** of **Training Review**.

3. Change the **Start date** by clicking the date selection icon, 🔲, to the right of the **Start date** box. From the date selection pane, click **Today**.

4. Change the **Due date** by clicking the date selection icon, 🔲, to the right of the Due date box and choosing a date 7 days from today.

Note: *Notice the **Information Bar** which informs you that the current task is **Due in 7 days**.*

5. Drop down the **Status** box and examine the various options available. As you have not started this task yet, select **Not Started** (the default).

6. Set the **Priority** to **High** and leave **% Complete** as **0%**.

7. Click once in the **Message Area** and enter **Review all training materials**.

8. To save the new task, click **Save & Close**. It appears as a new item on the **Task List**. Notice the **DUE DATE** that has been set.

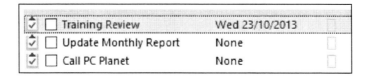

Exercise 58 - Task Views

Guidelines:

There are several ways of displaying the **Task List**:

- **Simple List**   Shows subject, categories and due date
- **Detailed**   Shows more columns such as priority, status and date completed
- **To-Do List**   Brief task details grouped by due date
- **Prioritized**   Tasks grouped by priority
- **Active**   A detailed list showing only active tasks
- **Completed**   A detailed list showing only completed tasks
- **Today**   A simple list showing only those tasks due today
- **Next 7 Days**   A detailed list showing tasks due in the next 7 days
- **Overdue**   A detailed list showing only overdue tasks

Actions:

1. Display the **VIEW** tab. Then, click **Change View** and examine the various different views that can be selected.

2. Click **Detailed** and observe the effect in the **Task List**. More columns showing more details are shown.

3. Click the **Change View** button again and select **To-Do List**. Tasks are grouped by due date. Select a task and its details appear in the **Reading Pane**.

4. Continue to experiment by selecting each of the views described above. Notice the effect in the **Task List** and consider how each displays and group tasks.

5. When you are finished, click the **Change View** button again and select **Simple List**.

*Note: Task information is also available on the **To-Do Bar**.*

6. Next, click the **To-Do Bar** button in the **Layout** group. From the options that appear, select **Tasks**.

7. Examine the **To-Do Bar** that appears. All of your tasks are shown in **To-Do List** format on the **To-Do Bar**.

*Note: You can also view tasks on the **To-Do Bar** in **Mail** view.*

8. Click the **To-Do Bar** button in the **Layout** group and select **Off** to hide the **To-Do Bar** again.

*Note: In the same way that you sorted messages in Exercise 48, you can also sort tasks in the **Task List** by clicking column headers.*

Exercise 59 - Editing Tasks

Guidelines:

Once you have created a task, it is very easy to edit and change it. In fact, as progress on a task changes, you are encouraged to return to and update its details in order to track progress.

Actions:

1. You should currently have 3 tasks in your **Task List**. Locate and double-click the **Training Review** task to edit it.

2. The detailed task window appears. You have made an early start on the training review today, so change the **Status** to **In Progress**.

3. Set the **% Complete** to **25%** (use the up spinner, ▲, or replace the value in the text box with **25** and press <**Enter**>).

Note: *Setting **% Complete** to **0%** will automatically change the **Status** to **Not Started**. Similarly, setting **% Complete** to **100%** will change the **Status** to **Complete**, and setting **% Complete** to anywhere in between will change the **Status** to **In Progress**.*

4. Change the **Due date** to 14 days time. Notice that the **Information Bar** changes.

5. You have decided that the training review is no longer an important task. Change the **Priority** to **Low**.

Note: *You can set reminders on upcoming or current tasks.*

6. Click the checkbox to the left of **Reminder**. Then, using the date selection icon, ▦, set a reminder for 7 days time at **12:00**.

7. Click **Save & Close** to save your changes.

8. Next, double-click the **Update Monthly Report** to edit it. Change its priority to **High** and **% Complete** to **50%** (notice that the task's **Status** automatically changes to **In Progress**). Set a **Due Date** of **Tomorrow**.

9. Click **Save & Close** to update this task.

Exercise 60 - Categorising Tasks

Guidelines:

Categories can be used to place tasks into colour-coded groups. This useful feature makes it easy to identify different types of task at a glance.

Note: Although less frequently used, you can also categorise e-mail messages using the same techniques described here.

Actions:

1. Double-click the **Update Monthly Report** task to start editing it. Then, click the **Categorize** button in the **Tags** group.

2. Select **All Categories** and the **Color Categories** dialog box appears.

3. Click **New** to add a new category. **Name** the new category **High Importance** and, using the **Color** drop-down, select **Red**. Click **OK**.

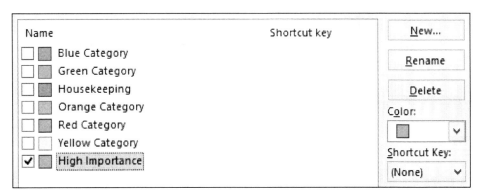

4. Click **OK** again and the selected task is placed in the new **High Importance** category. Notice the colour-coded banner that appears at the top of the task window.

5. Click **Save & Close**. The task now appears with a red category indicator.

6. Double-click the **Training Review** task. Then, click the **Categorize** button in the **Tags** group and select **All Categories**.

7. Create a **New** category and **Name** it **Low Importance**. **Color** this category **Green** and click **OK**.

Exercise 60 - Continued

8.   Click **OK** again and the selected task is placed in the new **Low Importance** category. Click **Save & Close**; it appears on the **Task List** with a green category indicator.

9.   Double-click **Call PC Planet** and place this task in a new category named **Office**. Make sure the **Office** category is coloured **Orange**.

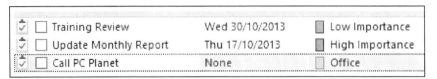

Note: Tasks can be placed in multiple categories.

10. Edit the **Update Monthly Report** task again. Then click the **Categorize** button, select **All Categories**, and place a tick in the checkbox to the left of the new **Office** category.

11. Click **OK** and the **Update Monthly Report** task now appears in both the **Office** and **High Importance** categories.

12. Click **Save & Close** and notice the effect in the **Task List**.

13. Click **New Task** in the **New** group to create a new task. Enter the **Subject** as **Replace Office Water Cooler** and select a **Due date** of tomorrow.

14. Click the **Categorize** button and select **All Categories**. Place this task in both the **Low Importance** and **Office** categories and click **OK**.

*Note: To remove a task from a category, simply use the **Categories** button.*

15. Click the **Categorize** button and select **All Categories**. Remove the tick in the checkbox to the left of the **Low Importance** category and click **OK**. The task now appears in a single category only.

16. Click **Save & Close**. The new, categorised task appears in the **Task List**.

*Note: Depending on your settings, you may also have a **Categorize** button on the **HOME** tab that can be used to add tasks to categories.*

Exercise 61 - Marking Tasks as Complete

Guidelines:

When you finish a task, you should mark it as complete. Completed tasks will remain in the **Task List** until they are deleted.

Actions:

1. Select the **Update Monthly Report** task in the **Task List**. You have just completed this activity and would now like to mark the task as complete.

2. Click the small **Complete** checkbox to the left of the task. It is marked with strikethrough as completed, but is not removed from the list.

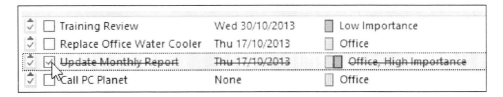

3. Click the **Complete** checkbox again for **Update Monthly Report**. The selected task is made active once more.

4. Double-click the **Update Monthly Report** task. Change the **Status** to **Completed** (notice the **% Complete** value automatically changes to **100%**).

5. Click **Save & Close** to close the task window. The task appears marked as complete again.

6. Display the **VIEW** tab and click the **Change View** button. Select **Active**. The completed **Update Monthly Report** task is not shown.

7. Click the **Change View** button again and select **Completed**. The **Update Monthly Report** task is the only one that appears.

8. Click **Change View** again and select **Simple List** to view all tasks.

Note: *Depending on your settings, you may also have a **Mark Complete** button on the **HOME** tab that can be used to mark tasks as complete.*

Exercise 62 - Assigning Tasks to Others

Guidelines:

Tasks can be assigned (delegated) to other people, who can either **Accept** or **Decline** them. An assigned task will also remain in your **Task List** so that progress can be monitored.

Actions:

1. Click **New Task** on the **HOME** tab to create a new task. Enter the **Subject** as **Prepare Financial Report** and select a **Due date** of tomorrow.

2. In the **Message Area** enter **Prepare the Financial Report for tomorrow's management meeting.**

3. This sounds like a perfect job for *Fiona Jones* at *Big Planet Support*. Let's assign this task to her...

4. With the the **TASK** tab displayed, click the **Assign Task** button in the **Manage Task** group.

5. In the **Message Area**, above the existing text, enter the following:

   Hi Fiona. Can you please complete this month's financial report?

6. In the **To** box enter the e-mail address: **fiona@bigplanetsupport.co.uk**

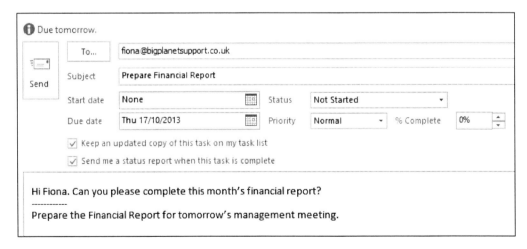

Note: Notice the two checkboxes boxes above the **Message Area**. The new task in your **Task List** will be kept updated as the recipient changes it and you will receive a message when it is finally marked as complete.

7. Click **Send**.

Note: Fiona will now receive an e-mail prompting her to **Accept** or **Decline** the task. Whichever choice she makes, you will receive a message in your **Inbox** and the task will be automatically updated as she changes it.

Exercise 63 - Outlook Today

Guidelines:

Outlook Today provides a summary of all mail, task and calendar items that are outstanding or due today.

Actions:

1. From the *Outlook* **Folder Pane**, click the **Mail** view button, .

2. Then, select the name of your mailbox on the **Folder Pane** (this will appear at the top of the **Folders List**).

3. The *Outlook Today* view appears. This features a summary of today's unread/unsent e-mail, flagged messages, outstanding tasks and calendar appointments (if applicable).

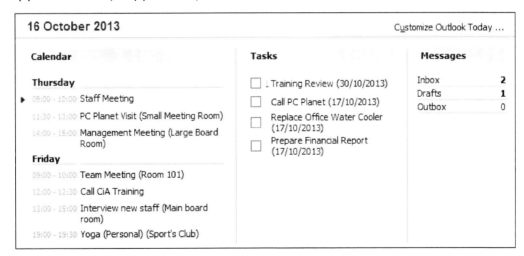

Note: *The screenshot above is provided for demonstration purposes only. The contents of your* Outlook Today *screen will appear differently.*

4. The information shown in *Outlook Today* can be changed. Click **Customize Outlook Today**. View the various options and then click **Cancel** to accept the default, recommended settings.

5. Finally, return to your **Inbox** folder by selecting it on the **Folders List**.

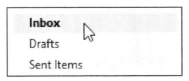

Exercise 64 - Deleting Tasks

Guidelines:

If you would like to delete an old or unwanted task, you can delete it from your **Task List**.

Note: *It is recommended that you mark finished tasks as complete rather than delete them. This provides you with a history that you can refer back to if needed.*

Actions:

1.   Click the **Tasks** view button, , at the bottom of the *Outlook* **Folder Pane**. The **Task** view appears.

Note: *If you cannot see the **Tasks** view button, click the **More** button, , and select **Tasks** from the menu that appears.*

2.   **Tasks** should still be selected under **My Tasks**. If it is not, select it now.

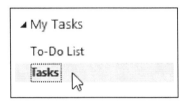

3.   Select the completed **Update Monthly Report** task in the **Task List**. Then, click **Remove from List** in the **Manage Task** group. The task is deleted.

Note: *Clicking **Delete** and **Remove from List** performs the same action.*

4.   Next, select **Prepare Financial Report**. Then click the **Delete** button. The task is deleted.

5.   Select **Replace Office Water Cooler**. Then press <**Delete**>. The task is deleted.

6.   By using **Delete** or **Remove from List**, remove **Call PC Planet** and **Training Review** from the **Task List**.

Note: *Deleted tasks are moved to the **Deleted Items** folder in **Mail** view. To restore a deleted task, simply move it back to the **Tasks** folder (as you learned in Exercise 50).*

Exercise 65 - Notes

Guidelines:

Outlook features tools to create "sticky" notes that are ideal for quickly recording a line or two of information. By default they are displayed in yellow, but the colour can be changed by assigning them to a new category.

Actions:

1. Click the **More** button, \[••• \], at the bottom of the *Outlook* **Folder Pane** and select **Notes** from the menu.

2. The **Notes** view appears. Click the **New Note** button on the **HOME** tab. An electronic note is created on the screen.

3. Enter the text **Water the office plants**.

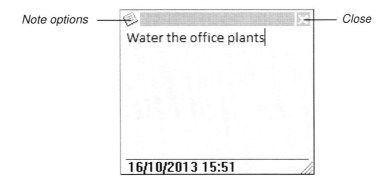

4. Click the **Close** button towards the top right corner of the note. It appears as an icon in the **Note List**.

5. To open and edit the note, double click its icon in the **Note List**.

6. Change the text to **Water the office flowers**.

Note:　*Depending on your settings, you may also be able to categorise a note in the same way that you categorise a task. If available, a **Categorize** button will appear in the **Tags** group.*

7. Close the note to save the changes. The note's icon text is updated.

8. Then, with the new note selected in the **Note List**, click the **Delete** button on the **HOME** tab (or press the <**Delete**> key on the keyboard). The note is removed.

Exercise 66 - Revision

Guidelines:

At the end of every section you get the chance to complete one or more revision exercises to develop your skills. You should aim to complete the following steps without referring back to the previous exercises.

Actions:

1. Open **Tasks** view.

2. Then, using the **New Task Box** box, quickly create a simple new task with the subject **Create Company Presentation**.

3. Next, click **New Task** in the **New** group to create a new task. Enter the **Subject** as **Arrange Team Building Day** and select a **Due date** of tomorrow.

4. Save and close the new task.

5. Place the **Create Company Presentation** task in the custom **Office** category.

6. Edit the **Arrange Team Building Day** task and select a **Start date** of today. Change the **Due date** to 7 days from now.

7. Change the **Priority** to **High** and set the **% Complete** to **25%**. Notice that the **Status** is automatically changed to **In Progress**.

8. Place the **Arrange Team Building Day** task in both the custom **Office** and **High Importance** categories.

9. Set a reminder to occur at **12:00** in two days time.

10. Save and close the task.

11. Mark the **Create Company Presentation** as complete.

12. Remove the **Create Company Presentation** from the **Task List**.

13. Select the **Arrange Team Building Day** task and view the **Color Categories** dialog box.

14. Delete the **High Importance**, **Low Importance** and **Office** categories.

15. Delete the **Arrange Team Building Day** task.

Section 11

Calendars

By the end of this section you should be able to:

Use Calendar View

Create an Appointment

Edit and Cancel an Appointment

Create Recurring Appointments

Create All Day Events

Invite Others to an Appointment

Accept or Reject an Invitation

Print a Schedule

Exercise 67 - Calendar

Guidelines:

Outlook features a handy **Calendar** tool. This can be used to plan your daily activities and schedule appointments and meetings with others.

Note: If you have permission, you can also view the calendars of other people in your organisation using the Calendar Selection Pane.

Actions:

1.   From the *Outlook* **Folder Pane**, click the **Calendar** view button, ▦.

2.   The **Calendar** view appears. Click the **Day** button in the **Arrange** group on the **Ribbon** (if it is not already selected).

3.   Notice that today's date is selected on the **Date Selection Pane** and shown in the **Calendar View Pane**.

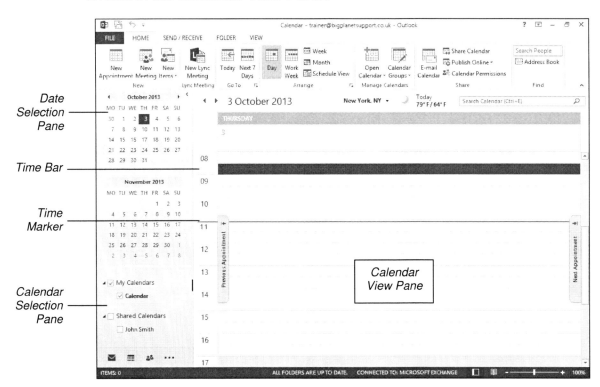

Note: Locate the Time Marker on the Time Bar. This indicates the current time and will gradually move downwards as the day progresses.

4.   Using the scrollbar, scroll the **Calendar View Pane** up and down. Notice that the standard "working day" (8am to 5pm) is shown in white, with time outside of this shaded.

5.   Leave your **Calendar** open for the next exercise.

Exercise 68 - Calendar Views

Guidelines:

The buttons in the **Arrange** group on the **Ribbon** allow you to view your **Calendar** by day, week or month. In **Day** view, each hour of the day is displayed in rows across the calendar creating a grid of 30 minute "time slots".

Note: The screenshots provided in this section are for illustrative purposes only. The dates and times selected will appear differently on your screen.

Actions:

1. Examine the **Date Selection Pane** and notice that today's date is currently highlighted (i.e. it appears in a blue box, as the example below demonstrates).

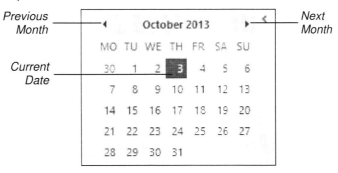

2. By clicking different dates on the **Date Selection Pane**, explore other dates in your **Calendar**. Observe the effect in the **Calendar View Pane**.

*Note: The **Previous Month** and **Next Month** buttons can be used to move between adjacent calendar months.*

3. Drag across two or more days on the **Date Selection Pane** and the **Calendar View Pane** will display them all side-by-side.

4. Go back to today's date by clicking **Today** in the **Go To** group.

5. Examine the buttons in the **Arrange** group. Select each of them in turn and observe the effect in the **Calendar View Pane**.

6. Select the **Day** button to return to a single day display.

7. Next, click the **Go To** dialog box launcher button, ⬚, in the **Go To** group.

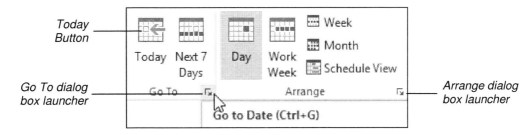

8. Examine the **Go To Date** dialog box that appears.

Exercise 68 - Continued

9. Click the drop-down arrow on the right of the **Date** box. A calendar similar to the **Date Select Pane** appears. Find and select the date for *next Monday*.

10. Click **OK** and next Monday appears in the **Calendar View Pane**. This is a useful technique for jumping directly to a date in the past or future.

11. Click the **Go To** dialog box launcher button again to display the **Go To Date** dialog box. In the **Date** box, replace the date text with your birthday.

Note: Dates can be entered in various styles, e.g. 4/4/1979, 4-4-79, 4-Apr-79.

12. Click **OK** and your birthday appears in the **Calendar View Pane**. What day of the week were you born on?

13. Go back to today's date by clicking the **Today** button.

*Note: Recall that a standard "working day" (8am to 5pm) is shown in white in the **Calendar View Pane**, with time outside of this shaded.*

14. The definition of a working day and working week can be changed. Click the **Arrange** group's dialog box launcher button, ⬜.

15. Examine the **Outlook Options** window that appears. **Work time** settings can be adjusted here to match your personal circumstances.

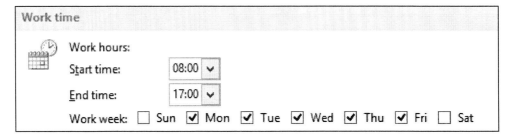

16. For now, click **Cancel** to keep *Outlook's* default, recommended settings.

Exercise 69 - Quick Appointments

Guidelines:

To quickly create a new appointment in your **Calendar**, simply select a time slot in the **Calendar View Pane** and enter the appointment's subject text.

Actions:

1. You have arranged a 30 minute staff meeting tomorrow at 2pm. So that you don't forget this appointment, let's enter the event into your **Calendar**…

2. First, using the **Date Selection Pane**, select <u>tomorrow's</u> date.

Note: Always check that a new appointment does not clash with a current event. Although Outlook allows overlapping appointments, you can't be in two places at once!

3. You have no other appointments in your diary at 2pm, so click once to select the **14:00** time slot (labelled as **14**) in the **Calendar View Pane**, as shown below. The time slot is highlighted.

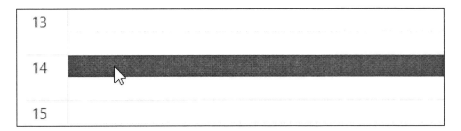

Note: Recall that each hour of the day is displayed in rows across the calendar, creating a grid of 30 minute time slots. You may need to scroll up and down to find a specific time of day.

4. To create a new appointment, simply start typing its subject text: **Staff Meeting**.

5. Press <**Enter**> to complete the new appointment. It will appear in the **Calendar View Pane**.

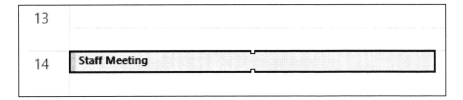

Note: A quick appointment is created with a default 15 minute reminder. You will learn more about reminders in the next exercise.

6. You have also arranged a 2 hour management meeting tomorrow at 4pm. Let's enter this event into your **Calendar** also.

Exercise 69 - Continued

7.   With tomorrow's date still selected and no other appointments at that time, click and drag to select the *four 30 minute* time slots between **16:00** and **18:00**, as shown below.

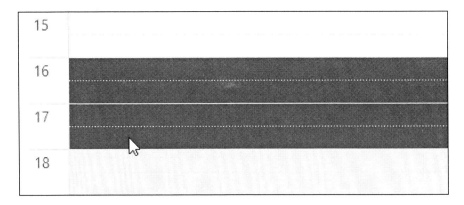

8.   Start typing its subject text: **Management Meeting**.

9.   Press <**Enter**> to complete the new appointment. It will appear in the **Calendar View Pane**.

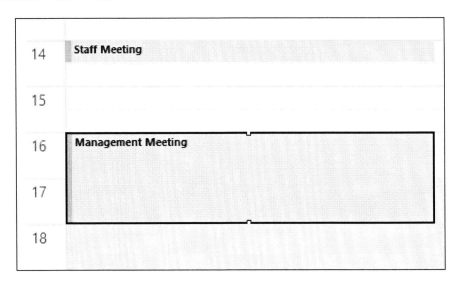

Note: *Notice that you can create appointments in both the working day (white time slots) and non-working day (shaded time slots).*

10. You now have two appointments scheduled for tomorrow. Leave the **Calendar** view open with tomorrow's date selected.

Note: *Similar to tasks, you can also place appointments into different categories. This will shade the appointment's background in the category's selected colour.*

Exercise 70 - Detailed Appointments

Guidelines:

A quick appointment is ideal for entering a basic event into your **Calendar**. However, for more control over the finer details of an appointment, *Outlook* features a variety of useful additional options and settings.

Note: *You can also choose to receive a useful **reminder** of an upcoming appointment in your **Calendar** (15 minutes before the event, by default).*

Actions:

1. You have arranged a one-hour visit to a local ICT supply company tomorrow at 10am. So that you don't forget this appointment, let's enter it into your **Calendar**…

2. First, make sure tomorrow's date is selected (and you have no other appointments that occur at the same time).

3. Display the **HOME** tab and click the **New Appointment** button in the **New** group to open an **Untitled Appointment** window.

4. Examine the options and settings available, then enter the **Subject** as **Visit PC Planet** and the **Location** as **31 High Street**.

5. Select a **Start time** of **10.00** and an **End time** of **11.00** (1 hour).

Note: *Tomorrow's date should appear automatically in the **Start time** and **End time** date boxes as this was the date selected on the **Calendar** when the appointment was created. You are free to change the dates here if necessary when creating your own appointments.*

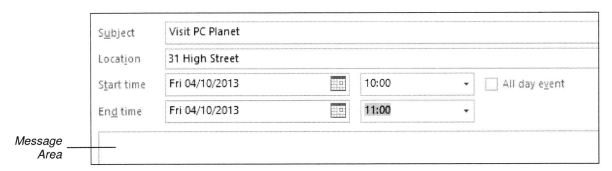

Note: *Make sure the **All day event** checkbox is <u>not</u> selected. As you will learn later, this is useful for creating **Calendar** entries that run all day and don't have a specific start or end time (i.e. days off).*

6. In the **Message Area**, enter the following <u>optional</u> text:

    Appointment with Miss Jones to discuss the purchase of new office computers.

7. Click the **Reminder** drop-down button in the **Options** group.

Exercise 70 - Continued

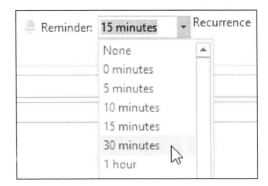

8. Change the default reminder time to **30 minutes**.

9. Locate the **Show As** drop-down button in the **Options** group (above the **Reminder** drop-down). By default, this currently reads **Busy**.

10. Click the **Show As** drop-down button and examine the various options available.

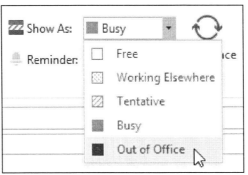

Note: *Appointment time can be designated as* ***Free*** *(white),* ***Working Elsewhere*** *(purple dots),* ***Tentative*** *(purple and white stripes),* ***Busy*** *(purple) or* ***Out of Office*** *(dark purple).*

11. As the appointment will be at *PC Planet*, select **Out of Office**.

12. Click **Save & Close** to create the new appointment and set the reminder. It appears as a new entry in the **Calendar**.

13. Notice the coloured bar that appears to the left of the appointment. This matches the purple **Out of Office** colour selected earlier.

Note: *A reminder, similar to that shown on page 46, will now "pop up" in Outlook half an hour before the appointment is scheduled to occur. You can cancel (**Dismiss**) the reminder or delay it (**Snooze**) for a period of time.*

14. Notice that tomorrow's date is now bold on the **Date Selection Pane**. This indicates that one or more appointments are present on that day.

Exercise 71 - Editing Appointments

Guidelines:

Once an appointment has been created, it is easy to edit and change it.

Actions:

1. Your meeting with *Miss Jones* at *PC Planet* has been rescheduled to start at **11.30**. It has also been extended to last until **13.00** and will now occur at your location (in your office's small meeting room).

2. To edit this appointment, make sure tomorrow's date is still selected on the **Date Selection Pane**.

3. Double click the **Visit PC Planet** appointment in the **10.00** time slot. The detailed appointment window will appear.

4. Change the **Subject** to **PC Planet Visit** and the **Location** to **Small Meeting Room**.

5. Then, change the **Start time** to **11.30** (notice the **End time** automatically changes to **12.30** to maintain the appointment's length). Change the **End time** to **13:00**.

6. Change the **Show As** setting from **Out of Office** to **Busy**.

7. As you no longer need to travel to the meeting, reduce the **Reminder** time to **5 minutes**.

8. Click the **Save & Close** button to update the appointment.

9. Next, locate the **Staff Meeting** appointment at **14:00**. You have decided to move this to 9am so click and drag it upwards to the **09:00** time slot.

10. With the 9am appointment selected, notice the two resize handles. Click and drag the lower handle down to extend the meeting to 1 hour.

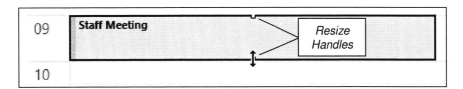

Exercise 71 - Continued

11. Using whichever technique you prefer, change the time of the **Management Meeting** to **14:00**. Reduce its length to 1 hour.

12. Add the location of the **Management Meeting** as **Large Board Room**, and set the **Reminder** to occur **10 minutes** before the event.

13. Your calendar should now appear as follows.

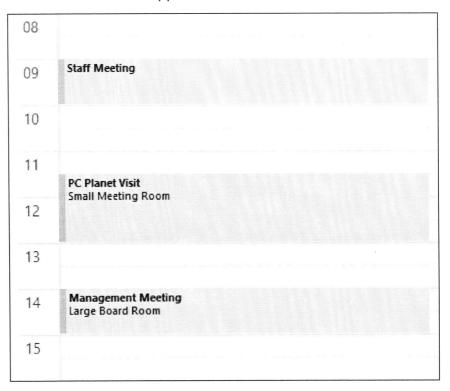

Note: *Appointment information is also available on the **To-Do Bar**.*

14. Display the **VIEW** tab and click the **To-Do Bar** button in the **Layout** group. From the options that appear, select **Calendar**.

15. Examine the **To-Do Bar** that appears, and select tomorrow's date on the date selection pane. All of that day's appointments are shown.

Note: *You can view appointments on the **To-Do Bar** in **Mail** and **Tasks** view.*

16. Click the **To-Do Bar** button in the **Layout** group and select **Off** to hide the **To-Do Bar** again.

17. Display the **HOME** tab.

Exercise 72 - Printing a Schedule

Guidelines:

Calendar details can be printed to show your appointments at a glance. They can be printed in various ways:

- **Daily Style**: the currently selected day with **Daily Task List** and **Notes**.

- **Weekly Agenda Style**: itemised appointments for each day of the selected week.

- **Weekly Calendar Style**: detailed grid of weekly appointments and times for the selected week.

- **Monthly Style**: itemised grid of the selected month's appointments.

- **Tri-fold Style**: the current day's appointments in detail with a **Daily Task List** and the seven day agenda.

- **Calendar Details Style**: a list of appointments in the selected period.

Actions:

1. Display the **FILE** tab and select **Print**.

2. Examine the various print-styles shown under **Settings**. Select each in turn and a preview is shown on the right.

Note: clicking the preview will zoom in/out.

3. Finally, select **Daily Style**.

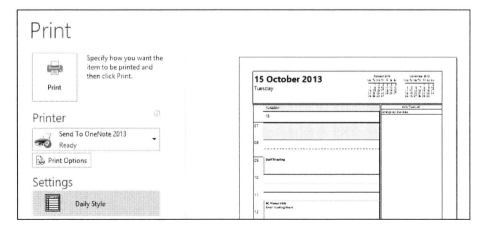

4. Select an *available* printer from the **Printer** drop-down list (your default printer will be automatically selected).

5. Click the large **Print** button to print a single copy of your calendar on the selected printer. You will automatically return to **Mail** view.

*Note: Alternatively, click the **Back** button to return without printing.*

Exercise 73 - Deleting Appointments

Guidelines:

If an appointment has been cancelled or is no longer required, you can delete it from your **Calendar**.

Actions:

1. Make sure tomorrow's date is still selected on the **Date Selection Pane**. The three appointments created in the previous exercise should be visible.

2. Select the **Staff Meeting** appointment in the **09:00** time slot by clicking it once.

*Note: Notice that the **APPOINTMENT** tab appears on the **Ribbon** and is automatically selected.*

3. Click the **Delete** button in the **Actions** group.

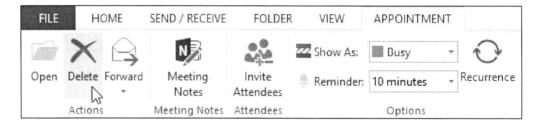

4. The appointment is deleted (and its reminder cancelled).

5. Next, select the **PC Planet Visit** appointment.

6. Press the <**Delete**> key on your keyboard to delete it.

7. Finally, using whichever technique you prefer, delete the **Management Meeting** appointment.

8. Leave the **Calendar** view open.

Exercise 74 - Recurring Appointments

Guidelines:

Individual appointments entered in the **Calendar** can be set to automatically repeat at regular intervals. This is useful for events that occur every day, week, month or year.

Note: *Although less frequently used, you can also create recurring tasks using the same techniques described here.*

Actions:

1. Starting tomorrow, you want to spend one hour each week learning to speak **Esparanto**. Let's enter this recurring event into your **Calendar**...

2. Make sure tomorrow's date is still selected on the **Date Selection Pane**.

3. Click the **New Appointment** button in the **New** group to open an **Untitled Appointment** window.

4. Enter the **Subject** as **Learn Esperanto** and the **Location** as **College**.

Note: *Make sure the **All day event** checkbox is <u>not</u> selected.*

5. Change the **Start time** to **18:00** and the **End time** to **19:00** (**1 hour**).

6. Next, click the **Recurrence** button in the **Options** group on the **APPOINTMENT** tab to open the **Appointment Recurrence** dialog box.

7. Select each of the **Recurrence pattern** settings (**Daily**, **Weekly**, **Monthly**, **Yearly**) in turn to see the range of recurrence options that can be used.

8. For this exercise, set the pattern to **Weekly** and make sure tomorrow's day is selected under **Recur every 1 week(s) on** (**Tuesday** is selected in the example below).

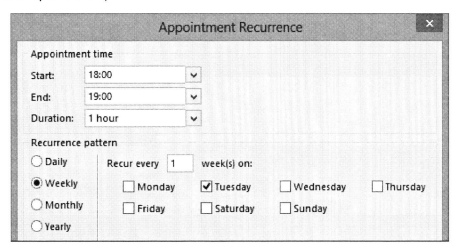

9. Notice the **Range of recurrence** settings. You can use these to define the start and end date of a recurring appointment.

Exercise 74 - Continued

10. For this exercise, create a never-ending event by selecting **No end date** (if it is not already selected).

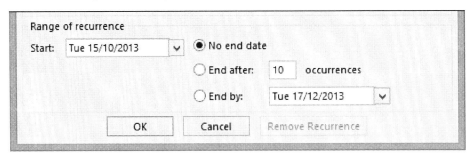

Note: *The example above shows a recurring appointment starting on Tuesday 15th October 2013. It has no end date.*

11. Click **OK**. The recurrence is indicated in the **Appointment** window.

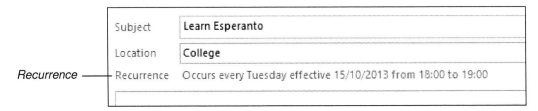

12. Click **Save & Close**.

13. Locate the new **Learn Esperanto** event in your **Calendar** and notice that the appointment appears with a recurrence symbol, ↻ .

14. Select **Month** from the **Arrange** group. The recurring appointment appears every week on the same day and time. This is known as a **series** of appointments.

15. Double click any of the scheduled **Learn Esperanto** appointments. You are given a choice to open this single appointment or the whole series.

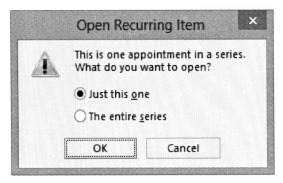

16. Select **The entire series** and click **OK**.

17. Select **Delete** from the **Actions** group to remove this recurring appointment. The entire series is removed.

18. Go back to today's date by clicking **Today** in the **Go To** group.

Exercise 75 - All Day Events

Guidelines:

Certain appointments do not need a specific start or end time, such as birthdays, holidays or full days spent working on a task. These are known as **All day events** and are a special kind of appointment in *Outlook*.

Note: *All day events do not appear on the **To-Do Bar** and are designated as **Free** time (rather than **Busy**).*

Actions:

1.   You have booked a last minute holiday to Spain and will be leaving today for one week. Let's enter this into your **Calendar**...

2.   Click the **Day** button in the **Arrange** group. Then make sure today's date is currently selected on the **Date Selection Pane**.

3.   Click the **New Appointment** button in the **New** group to open an **Untitled Appointment** window.

4.   Enter a **Subject** of **Holiday** and a **Location** of **Spain**.

5.   Notice that, by default, the **Start time** and **End time** for the event is set to the currently selected date (today).

6.   Change the **End time** by clicking the date selection icon, ▦, and choosing a date 7 days from today.

7.   To mark this appointment as an all day event, place a tick in the **All day event** checkbox.

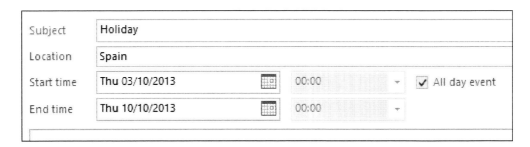

8.   You don't need to be reminded of this event, so change **Reminder** to **None**. Then, click **Save & Close** to add the event to the **Calendar**.

Exercise 75 - Continued

9. Notice the **All day event** that appears at the top of the **Calendar**. Explore the various views available in the **Arrange** group to see how this event spans across multiple days.

10. Select the **Day** button in the **Arrange** group to return to a single day display.

11. Then, make sure today's date is selected by clicking **Today** in the **Go To** group.

12. Select the **Holiday** event in the **Calendar View Pane** by clicking it once.

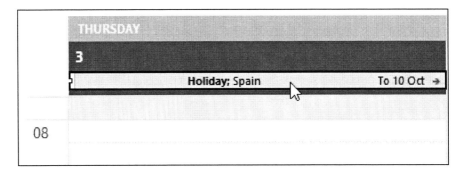

13. Then, using whichever technique you prefer, delete the event.

14. Leave the **Calendar** view open.

Exercise 76 - Organising a Meeting

Guidelines:

The **Calendar** can be used to arrange and co-ordinate meetings with other people. Invitations are then sent to attendees by e-mail and recipients can either **Accept**, **Decline** or **Tentatively** respond.

Note: *Contacts in your **Address Book** can be asked to attend meetings that you organise. They can be invited as a **Required** (must come) or as an **Optional** attendee.*

Actions:

1.   You are planning a meeting with two colleagues, *Fiona* and *Hassan,* to discuss the purchase and installation of a new printer. To set up and agree on a meeting time, click the **New Meeting** button in the **New** group.

2.   An **Untitled Meeting** window appears. Examine the various options and settings available on this screen.

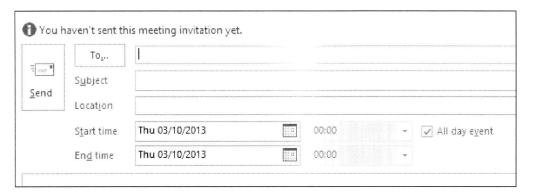

3.   Click the **To** button, 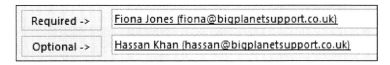, to open your **Address Book**. Make sure **Contacts** is selected in the **Address Book** drop-down.

4.   As the printer is for *Fiona*, she is required to attend the meeting. Select *Fiona Jones* and click the **Required** button.

5.   *Hassan* will install the new printer and *may* wish to attend the meeting if he wants to. Select **Hassan Khan** and click the **Optional** button.

| Required -> | Fiona Jones (fiona@bigplanetsupport.co.uk) |
| Optional -> | Hassan Khan (hassan@bigplanetsupport.co.uk) |

6.   Click **OK**.

7.   Enter the **Subject** as **Printer Meeting**.

8.   Enter the **Location** as **Small Meeting Room**.

Exercise 76 - Continued

Note: If using Outlook *on a compatible network, a **Rooms** button and **Room Finder** may appear. This can be used to check the availability of and reserve a room in your organisation for the duration of a meeting. Other resources such as cars and equipment can also be reserved.*

9.   Make sure the **All day event** checkbox is <u>not</u> selected, and then arrange for the meeting to occur <u>tomorrow</u> from **14:30** to **15:30** (**1 hour**).

10.   In the **Message Area**, enter the following invitation text:

   Hi Fiona and Hassan,

   I've arranged a meeting tomorrow to discuss Fiona's new printer. I look forward to seeing you there.

11.   Notice that a default **Reminder** of **15 minutes** has been automatically set in the **Options** group.

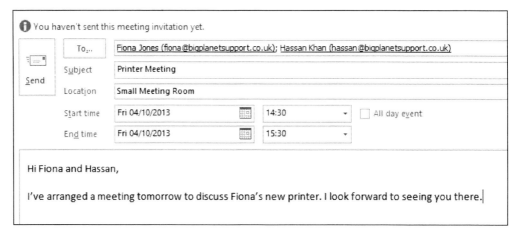

Note: If using Outlook *on a compatible network, the **Scheduling Assistant/ Scheduling** button in the **Show** group can be used to compare your calendars and select a commonly suitable time.*

12.   Click **Send** to send out invitations by e-mail.

Note: As the organiser of a meeting you are automatically invited. You will not receive an invitation e-mail.

13.   Notice that the new meeting appointment, including who has organised it, is now shown for tomorrow's date on the **Calendar View Pane**.

14.   Leave *Outlook* open for the next exercise.

Exercise 77 - Meeting Invitations

Guidelines:

Recipients of an e-mail invitation can **Accept** or **Decline** the request to attend, state they are **Tentative** (unsure), or propose a new time. Their replies will be sent back to you by e-mail and their decision shown in your calendar.

Actions:

1.   From the *Outlook* **Folder Pane**, click the **Mail** view button, . Then, select the **Sent Items** folder in the **Folders List**.

2.   Find the **Printer Meeting** message in the **Message List**. Select this to examine the e-mail invitation that was automatically sent to *Fiona* and *Hassan* in the previous exercise.

3.   Notice the inactive **Accept**, **Tentative**, **Decline**, and **Propose New Time** buttons that appear at the top of the message in the **Reading Pane**.

Note: As the **Printer Message** invitation was sent to others, you are prevented from responding on their behalf. However, the recipient will see the following:

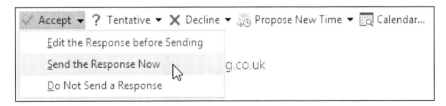

Note: When you **Accept** (or "tentatively accept") an invitation, the invitation e-mail will be automatically removed from your **Inbox** and will appear as an appointment on your **Calendar**. If you **Decline**, it will simply be removed from your **Inbox**.

Note: An automatic response e-mail is created and sent to a meeting's organiser when you reply to an invitation. You can edit this by selecting **Edit the Response before Sending**, or prevent it by selecting **Do Not Send a Response**. You can even suggest a new time by clicking **Propose New Time**.

Exercise 78 - Removing Attendees

Guidelines:

It is easy to add or remove attendees from a meeting that has already been organised. This sends update messages to everyone affected by the change.

Note: *Only the organiser of a meeting can add or remove attendees.*

Note: *If using* Outlook *on a compatible network, the* **Rooms** *button can be used to cancel rooms that may have been reserved. If applicable, other reserved resources such as cars and equipment can also be cancelled.*

Actions:

1.   From the *Outlook* **Folder Pane**, click the **Calendar** view button, 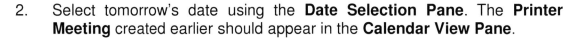.

2.   Select tomorrow's date using the **Date Selection Pane**. The **Printer Meeting** created earlier should appear in the **Calendar View Pane**.

3.   Click **Printer Meeting** once to select it (scheduled to occur at **14:30**). The **MEETING** tab is automatically selected.

4.   Click the **Add or Remove Attendees** button in the **Attendees** group to open your **Address Book**. Make sure **Contacts** is selected in the **Address Book** drop-down.

5.   *Hassan* will not be required to attend the meeting after all. Click once to select **Hassan Khan** in the **Optional** box.

Required ->	Fiona Jones (fiona@bigplanetsupport.co.uk)
Optional ->	Hassan Khan (hassan@bigplanetsupport.co.uk)

6.   Press <**Delete**> to remove this attendee.

Note: *You can also add new attendees using the techniques described in exercise 76*

7.   Click **OK** to confirm the change. Then, click **Send Update**. Examine the dialog box that appears.

Exercise 78 - Continued

8.   By default, only the attendees added or removed from a meeting will receive an update e-mail. Click **OK**.

9.   From the *Outlook* **Folder Pane**, click the **Mail** view button. Then, select the **Sent Items** folder in the **Folders List**.

10.   Find the **Canceled: Printer Meeting** message in the **Message List**. Select this to examine the e-mail invitation that was sent to *Hassan*.

Note: *For the recipients of a meeting update, clicking* **Remove from Calendar** *will automatically remove the meeting from their* **Calendar**.

11.   From the *Outlook* **Folder Pane**, click the **Calendar** view button.

Exercise 79 - Cancelling a Meeting

Guidelines:

To delete a meeting where invitations have already been sent, you must cancel it. This sends meeting cancellation messages to all attendees informing them of the change.

Note: Only the organiser of a meeting can cancel it.

Actions:

1.   Select tomorrow's date using the **Date Selection Pane**. The **Printer Meeting** created earlier should appear in the **Calendar View Pane**.

2.   Click the **Printer Meeting** appointment once to select it (scheduled to occur at **14:30**). The **MEETING** tab appears and is automatically selected.

3.   Click the **Cancel Meeting** button in the **Actions** group.

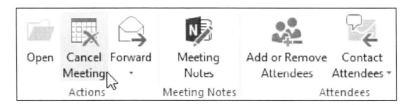

4.   Examine the window that appears.

5.   To cancel the meeting, click **Send Cancellation**. All attendees of the meeting will receive a cancellation update e-mail.

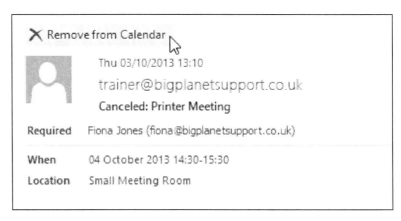

6.   The meeting is removed from your **Calendar**.

*Note: For the recipients of a meeting cancellation update, clicking **Remove from Calendar** will automatically remove the meeting from their Calendar.*

7.   Go back to today's date by clicking **Today** in the **Go To** group on the **HOME** tab.

Exercise 80 - Revision

Guidelines:

At the end of every section you get the chance to complete one or more revision exercises to develop your skills. You should aim to complete the following steps without referring back to the previous exercises.

Actions:

1. In **Calendar** view, create a three hour appointment for *next* Monday at 9 am. It is to interview new job applicants and will take place in your office's Interview Suite.

1. You should set a reminder for 30 minutes before the appointment.

2. Create an all day event for Friday *next* week: a team building exercise at the local army assault course. Complete the relevant details and mark the time as "Out of Office".

3. Organise a 30 minute "staff meeting" for *next* Wednesday at 1pm. Invite *Fiona* and *Hassan*. It will take place in the small meeting room.

4. Cancel the meeting and send cancellation updates.

5. Find and delete the two remaining appointments created in this exercise.

6. Go to your next birthday and create an all day event to mark it.

Note: *You will now delete any appointments, contacts, tasks, distribution lists or e-mail messages created during this guide.*

7. Go to **Contacts** view and delete the contacts for *Fiona* and *Hassan*.

8. Return to your **Mail** view and delete any e-mail messages created and received during this guide.

9. Empty your **Deleted Items** folder.

10. Close *Outlook*.

Answers

Exercise 7

2.   Outlook is a Personal Information Management (PIM) tool. It is used to send, receive and organise e-mail messages and manage contacts and calendar appointments.

3.   @ is pronounced "at".

4.   An organisation's domain name.

5.   The view buttons on the Folder Pane can be used to switch between Outlook views.

6.   All new e-mail messages that you receive are placed in your Inbox folder.

7.   The Message List shows all messages contained in a folder. Different folders can be selected in the Folders List.

8.   The content of any message selected in the Message List is previewed in the Reading Pane.

Exercise 16

4.   All recipients of a message can see who it was from and who it was sent to, including any carbon copies. However, recipients will not see the addresses of people who receive a blind carbon copy.

Other Products from CiA Training

CiA Training is a leading publishing company which has consistently delivered the highest quality products since 1985. Our experienced in-house publishing team has developed a wide range of flexible and easy to use self-teach resources for individual learners and corporate clients all over the world.

Supporting many popular qualifications including ECDL, CLAIT, ITQ and Functional Skills, our products are an invaluable asset to tutors and training managers seeking support for their programme delivery.

At the time of publication our range includes:

- **ITQ Level 1, Level 2 and Level 3**

- **New CLAIT, CLAIT Plus and CLAIT Advanced**

- **ECDL**

- **ECDL Advanced**

- **Functional Skills**

- **Cambridge Nationals**

- **Start IT**

- **Skill for Life**

- **CiA Revision Series**

- **Open Learning Guides**

- **Trainers Packs**

- **And much, much more...**

Note: CiA Training learning resources are available in individual printed book format or as a site licence in PDF or editable Microsoft Word format.

We hope you have enjoyed using this guide and would love to hear your opinions about our materials. To let us know how we are doing and to get up-to-the-minute information about our current range of products, please visit us online at:

www.ciatraining.co.uk

Index